BIRDS of the ADIRONDACKS

A FIELD GUIDE

Alan E. Bessette
William K. Chapman
Warren S. Greene
Douglas R. Pens

North Country Books, Inc.
Utica, New York

Copyright © 1993
by
Alan E. Bessette
and
William K. Chapman

ISBN 0-932052-94-0

All Rights Reserved

No part of this book may be reproduced in any
manner without the written permission of the publisher
except for brief quotes for review purposes.

Cover Photo: Northern Saw-whet Owl, *Aegolius acadius*

Library of Congress Cataloging-in-Publication Data

Birds of the Adirondacks : a field guide / Alan Bessette . . . [et al].
    p. cm.
  Includes indexes.
  ISBN 0-932052-94-0
  1. Birds—New York (State)—Adirondack Mountains—Iden-
tification. 2. Birds—New York (State)—Adirondack Mountains
—Pictorial works.
  I. Bessette, Alan.
  QL684.N7B52 1992
  598.29747—dc20   91-42111
                                   CIP

North Country Books, Inc.
PUBLISHER—DISTRIBUTOR
18 Irving Place
Utica, New York 13501

TABLE OF CONTENTS

ACKNOWLEDGMENTS

Many people have made this field guide possible. We thank Valerie Conley for typing and proofing the manuscript and contributing to the quality of this work. We thank Arleen Bessette for reading the manuscript, providing technical assistance and making valuable suggestions for improving the book. Wayne Palmer and Larry Watkins provided useful historical data and assisted with the research efforts. We gratefully acknowledge the assistance provided by Barbara Loucks and Peter Nye of the Endangered Species Unit of the New York State Department of Environmental Conservation. They provided current data on the status of eagle and Peregrine Falcon populations in the Adirondack Park and information concerning the restoration programs for these birds.

Several of the photographs of species that are rare or extremely difficult to approach in the wild were taken of birds under the protection of professional caregivers, most of whom are licensed wildlife rehabilitators in New York State. The people to whom we owe this debt of special thanks are: Judy Cusworth of Woodhaven Wildlife Center, Peter Dubacker of Berkshire Bird Paradise Nature Center, Dave Wadell, Rick West, Lester Blauvelt, and Tom and Audrey Voss. We also wish to thank Dr. David Gapp and Dr. William Pfitsch of the Hamilton College Biology Department for allowing the photography of the passenger pigeon.

Warren Greene wishes to extend his personal acknowledgments to his wife Jeanne for her patience and support, and to Brian Henry for his constant companionship and encouragement over the years. Doug Pens also expresses his gratitude to his wife Eileen and to Dr. John Gustafson and Dr. Eugene Waldbauer, retired professors from the State University of New York at Cortland, for their inspirational guidance.

We thank Audrey Sherman for typesetting and making useful suggestions for improving the manuscript. We are grateful to John Mahaffy for designing the book, and for providing the drawings found throughout the text. We especially thank Sheila Orlin and Robert Igoe for their guidance and creativity, and for giving us the opportunity to write this book.

CREDITS

The authors and the staff at North Country Books wish to extend their sincere appreciation to the following photographers for allowing their work to appear in this guide. We also thank all other photographers who submitted additional material for consideration.

Warren S. Greene: Cover Photo; Pl. 2, No. 2; Pl. 5, No. 2, 3 & 4; Pl. 6, No. 1, 3 & 4; Pl. 7, No. 1, 3 & 4; Pl. 9, No. 2; Pl. 10, No. 1 & 2; Pl. 11, No. 3; Pl. 16, No. 3; Pl. 20, No. 1 & 3; Pl. 21, No. 1; Pl. 22, No. 2; Pl. 23, No. 3; Pl. 24, No. 1, 3 & 4; Pl. 25, No. 1, 2 & 4; Pl. 27, No. 1; Pl. 28, No. 3 & 4; Pl. 29, No. 1, 2 & 3; Pl. 30, No. 2 & 4; Pl. 31, No. 2 & 4; Pl. 32, No. 1, 3 & 4; Pl. 33, No. 1 & 4; Pl. 34, No. 1, 2 & 3; Pl. 35, No. 1; Pl. 37, No. 2 & 3; Pl. 38, No. 2 & 4; Pl. 39, No. 1; Pl. 41, No. 2 & 4; Pl. 42, No. 2; Pl. 43, No. 1, 3, & 4; Pl. 44, No. 1, 2, 3 & 4; Pl. 45, No. 1, 2, 3 & 4; Pl. 46, No. 2 & 3.

William Kent Chapman: Pl. 1, No. 1 & 4; Pl. 3, No. 2 & 4; Pl. 4, No. 1 & 4; Pl. 5, No. 1; Pl. 6, No. 2; Pl. 7, No. 2; Pl. 8, No. 3; Pl. 9, No. 1 & 4; Pl. 10, No. 3 & 4; Pl. 11, No. 1 & 2; Pl. 12, No. 2, 3 & 4; Pl. 13, No. 1; Pl. 15, No. 4; Pl. 16, No. 4; Pl. 17, No. 3; Pl. 21, No. 3; Pl. 22, No. 1 & 4; Pl. 23, No. 2; Pl. 26, No. 1.

Paul E. Meyers: Pl. 4, No. 2 & 3; Pl. 13, No. 4; Pl. 18, No. 1 & 4; Pl. 19, No. 1; Pl. 23, No. 4; Pl. 26, No. 2; Pl. 33, No. 3; Pl. 34, No. 4; Pl. 38, No. 3; Pl. 39, No. 3; Pl. 40, No. 1; Pl. 42, No. 3.

Dave Spier: Pl. 2, No. 1; Pl. 8, No. 4; Pl. 16, No. 1; Pl. 19, No. 3 & 4; Pl. 20, No. 4; Pl. 26, No. 4; Pl. 27, No. 2; Pl. 28, No. 1; Pl. 30, No. 1; Pl. 31, No. 3; Pl. 36, No. 3; Pl. 37, No. 4; Pl. 46, No. 1.

Gary VanRiper: Pl. 21, No. 2; Pl. 24, No. 2; Pl. 27, No. 3 & 4; Pl. 32, No. 2; Pl. 35, No. 2; Pl. 36, No. 2; Pl. 40, No. 2 & 3; Pl. 42, No. 1 & 4.

Marie Read: Pl. 15, No. 3; Pl. 17, No. 4; Pl. 18, No. 2 & 3; Pl. 25, No. 3; Pl. 33, No. 2; Pl. 35, No. 4; Pl. 36, No. 1; Pl. 37, No. 1.

David M. Bessette: Pl. 14, No. 2, 3 & 4; Pl. 15, No. 1; Pl. 17, No. 1 & 2.

Dorothy Crumb: Pl. 15, No. 2; Pl. 19, No. 2; Pl. 38, No. 1; Pl. 39, No. 4; Pl. 40, No. 4.

Monte Loomis: Pl. 21, No. 4; Pl. 23, No. 1; Pl. 28, No. 2; Pl. 30, No. 3; Pl. 36, No. 4; Pl. 41, No. 3.

Alan E. Bessette: Pl. 1, No. 3; Pl. 12, No. 1; Pl. 13, No. 2; Pl. 14, No. 1; Pl. 16, No. 2.

Leonard Lee Rue, III: Pl. 2, No. 3; Pl. 3, No. 1; Pl. 46, No. 4.

Mike Hopiak, Cornell Laboratory of Ornithology: Pl. 11, No. 4; Pl. 43, No. 2.

Douglas R. Pens: Pl. 26, No. 3; Pl. 31, No. 1.

Valerie Conley: Pl. 8, No. 2; Pl. 9, No. 3.

Betty D. Cottrille, Cornell Laboratory of Ornithology: Pl. 41, No. 1.

Bill Dyer, Cornell Laboratory of Ornithology: Pl. 39, No. 2.

Gary Lee: Pl. 13, No. 3.

Anne McGrath: Pl. 29, No. 4.

W. A. Paff, Cornell Laboratory of Ornithology: Pl. 20, No. 2.

Joe Platt, Cornell Laboratory of Ornithology: Pl. 2, No. 4.

Walter R. Spofford, Endangered Species Unit of NYS Dept. of Conservation: Pl. 1, No. 2.

Mary Tremaine, Cornell Laboratory of Ornithology: Pl. 35, No. 3.

Frederick Kent Truslow, Cornell Laboratory of Ornithology: Pl. 3, No. 3.

L. B. Wales, Cornell Laboratory of Ornithology: Pl. 8, No. 1.

Ernest Williams: Pl. 22, No. 3.

INTRODUCTION

This book is a field guide to those birds found in the Adirondack area. While a handful of specialized species may be encountered in only a few remote mountain habitats, the majority of the birds in this guide can be found throughout New York State and the entire northeast. Our first task in producing this work was to compile a species list. After much debate we decided to limit this book to those species that fall into at least one of the following three categories: 1) species that may be commonly encountered throughout the park, 2) species whose New York State range or breeding habitat is largely limited to the Adirondack area (this includes birds such as the Bald and Golden Eagles, the Peregrine Falcon, the Loon, the Spruce Grouse, the Three-toed Woodpecker, the Common Raven, the Gray Jay, the Boreal Chickadee, the Ruby-crowned Kinglet, the Northern Parula and the Cape May Warbler), 3) species such as the Cattle Egret and Black Vulture that are recent or uncommon visitants, but which we believe will become increasingly common in the near future. As much as space permitted we also included such high profile rare visitants as the northern owls, but in the end we had to eliminate birds such as the American White Pelican. While we found it fascinating that this unusual Rocky Mountain waterbird makes an occasional Adirondack appearance, we decided that such a rare occurrence fell outside the scope of this field guide. Equally frustrating was the process of keeping the comments section down to a reasonable size. As fascinating as historical data frequently is, in most cases we had to limit our comments to the field of natural history.

The primary objectives of this field guide are to aid in the identification of birds and to provide insights into aspects of avian natural history such as nesting behaviors and seasonal status. The size of this book makes it easy to carry along on hikes, camping trips or other outdoor activities.

ARRANGEMENT OF THE BOOK

The arrangement of this book is a continuation of traditions established by the previous Adirondack Field Guides in this series. Information is presented on the physical description, habitat, reproduction and seasonal status of each species. A section on comments gives additional information.

This book is a field guide and, like all field guides, its primary purpose is to assist readers in identifying whatever species they may encounter. To aid in this process the species descriptions are divided into large, easily recognized categories such as birds of prey and waterfowl. Under the largest category, the perching birds, species are further grouped according to their predominant color for easy identification.

Common name: The first information given for each bird species is its common name. This is the name that will be best known to the general population. Be cautious of relying too heavily on common names; in the case of similar species such as sparrows, local common names may be inaccurate or repetitive.

Scientific name: The scientific name indicated for each species is unique—only one species will have this name. Each scientific name is made up of two words. The first of these designates the genus, and indicates to what other species it may be closely related. The second word is the species designation, and this may not be shared by any other member of the same genus. Scientific names are usually given in Latin and are consistent throughout the world.

Overall color: This gives the predominant colors of the bird. It allows the reader to more rapidly identify any bird under the major categories. With some perching birds such as the robin, the upper and lower body have sharply contrasting colors. In these situations, the upper body color, including the wings, was used to determine the placement within color groups.

Plate: Each photograph has been selected for aesthetic qualities and identification characteristics. Every attempt has been made to include a representative photograph of each group of birds found in the Adirondack Park. The bird's scientific name, common name, and page number of the corresponding description have been provided beneath each photograph. Unless otherwise noted, photographs are of adult males.

Measurements: Average body measurements are included for each species to aid in identification. The length, as used in this book, is the distance from the tip of the bill to the tip of the tail. The wingspan is the distance between the tips when the wings are fully extended.

Description: The description gives vital identification characteristics such as coloration and shape of key body parts such as eyes, throat, bill, etc. when useful in the identification process. Color descriptions are for adult birds in the spring and summer. If different for other seasons, it is noted. For visitant species, the colors described are representative of their plumage while in the Adirondacks.

Nesting season: The nesting season lists the dates when eggs may be found in the nest. If the information indicates that a second brood or multiple broods may occur, the dates given are for the first brood.

Nest: The information presented in this section includes the location, composition and construction of the nest.

Eggs: This section gives the typical range for the number of eggs, their color and size.

Seasonal status: Information included here gives the seasons when each species is typically present in the Adirondacks.

Habitat: This gives the environment in which this bird is typically found. Many species will also visit urban areas when food sources such as feeders become available.

Similar species: Birds which are closely related or that closely resemble the described species and are also known to occur in the Adirondacks are briefly discussed in this section. Carefully compare any unknown specimen to the principal and similar species before making a final decision about its identification. Following the scientific name of each similar species is a parenthesis containing information about the season(s) during which that species may typically be observed in the Adirondacks. The seasonal abbreviations used are— Sp - spring; S - summer; F - fall; W - winter, and AS - all seasons.

Comments: Comments can include any interesting or useful information not covered by the previous sections.

Section I
Birds of Prey

Red-tailed Hawk
Buteo jamaicensis

Birds of Prey

The birds of prey includes eagles, ospreys, hawks, falcons, and vultures. They are known as meat-eaters, having stout hooked bills and long, sharp, deeply curved talons. Each category of the birds of prey has specific characteristics. Eagles and ospreys generally resemble hawks but are much larger and have proportionately longer wings. Hawks are typically divided into buteos, accipiters, and harriers. Buteos have broad rounded wings and broad rounded tails. They have distinctively marked tails which are a key feature for identification. Accipiters have broad rounded wings and long narrow tails. Harriers generally resemble accipiters but have longer, rounded wings. Falcons appear very streamlined with long pointed wings and long narrow tails. Vultures have long, broad, rounded wings and are easily differentiated from all other birds of prey by their featherless heads.

EAGLES

BALD EAGLE — Dark brown and white
Haliaeetus leucocephalus — Plate 1, No. 1
Length: 27-35 inches
Wingspan: 71-89 inches

Description Male: Upper body, lower body and wings dusky brown to dark brown. Head and neck white; bill stout, hooked downward, yellow. Tail white. Legs covered halfway down with dusky brown feathers; lower legs and toes yellow.

Description Female: Nearly identical to male.

Nesting Season: March - April.

Nest: Located high in a tree, large and bulky, loosely constructed of large sticks and branches. In 1989, several Bald Eagles successfully nested in the Adirondacks for the first time in about three decades. This population is a direct result of the successful restoration program carried out by the NYS Department of Conservation. In 1991 there were four active nests in the Adirondacks, and it is assumed that this number will grow as more of the previously released birds reach breeding age.

Eggs: Two to three, white to dirty white, 2.9 inches long by 2.2 inches wide.

Seasonal Status: Aside from the resident population, Bald Eagles from other areas migrate through the Adirondacks during each spring and fall.

Habitat: Wooded areas near large bodies of water.

Similar Species: The Golden Eagle, *Aquila chrysaetos* (Sp, S, F), also has dusky brown plumage but this extends over the entire body including the head, tail, and entire length of the legs. In addition, it has a grayish, hooked bill. The young Bald Eagle also has a grayish bill but lacks white head, neck and tail feathers, making these two species difficult to differentiate.

Comments: Has a reputation for stealing fish from ospreys, although just as often ospreys attack and harass eagles. The Bald Eagle has one of the largest wingspans of any bird in the Adirondacks, measuring six to nearly seven and one-half feet.

GOLDEN EAGLE
Aquila chrysaetos
Length: 30-41 inches
Wingspan: 78-92 inches

Brown
Plate 1, No. 2

Description Male: Upper body and wings dusky brown to dark brown with a slight golden iridescence. Lower body brown to dusky brown. Head and neck golden brown; bill stout, hooked downward, grayish. Tail dusky brown to dark brown, darkest at the tip. Legs covered with dusky brown feathers; toes yellow.

Description Female: Nearly identical to male.

Nesting Season: Uncertain.

Nest: Located on remote cliff ledges or high in trees, loosely constructed of sticks and branches. The Golden Eagle has only rarely nested in New York State during this century. The only successful nestings were recorded from 1957 to 1970.

Eggs: Two, dirty white with chestnut spotting, 2.91 inches long by 2.32 inches wide.

Seasonal Status: Spring, summer and fall.

Habitat: Large meadows and edges of woodlands on remote hills and mountains.

Similar Species: The Bald Eagle, *Haliaeetus leucocephalus* (AS), also has dusky brown plumage but has a white head and tail. Immature Bald Eagles lack the white head and tail, and have only their upper legs covered with feathers.

Comments: The Golden Eagle is primarily a hunter of remote open areas. With the reforestation of the Adirondacks, the amount of prime habitat available to this species has been greatly reduced.

THE OSPREY

OSPREY
Pandion haliaetus
Length: 22-24 inches
Wingspan: 54-72 inches

Dark brown
Plate 1, No. 3

Description Male: Upper body dusky brown to dark grayish brown, sometimes appearing nearly black. Lower body white, usually with a few brown streaks on the breast. Head mostly white, with a conspicuous dark brown eye bar and slight brown streaking on crown; bill hooked downward, bluish black. Wings long, dusky brown to dark grayish brown; in flight a large black spot is clearly visible midway on the leading edge of the wing. Tail narrowly fan-shaped, dark brown with thin white tip and several nearly black bands. Legs: upper leg covered with white feathers; lower leg and toes rough, bluish gray.

Description Female: Similar to male but usually with more pronounced breast streaking, sometimes forming an imperfect band.

Nesting Season: May - July.

Nest: Located high, typically in a dead tree, usually near water, large and bulky, loosely constructed of branches, lined with bark and grasses.

Eggs: Two to four, dirty white with irregular reddish brown blotches, 2.48 inches long by 1.75 inches wide.

Seasonal Status: Spring, summer and fall.

Habitat: Near rivers and lakes.

Similar Species: The Rough-legged Hawk, *Buteo lagopus* (AS), shares the conspicuous black wing spot of the Osprey, but differs by having a brown belly and a broader, darker, terminal tail band. The Bald Eagle, *Haliaeetus leucocephalus* (AS), is larger, has a dusky brown lower body and yellow feet, but lacks the broad, dark brown to nearly black eye bar.

Comments: Excellent fishing skills. Feeds mainly on fish.

THE HAWKS

ROUGH-LEGGED HAWK

Buteo lagopus

Length: 20-23 inches

Wingspan: 52-56 inches

Brown

Plate 1, No. 4

Description Male: Upper body feathers dark brown with pale edges. Lower body: breast dingy white, heavily streaked and spotted with dark brown; belly brown, usually white near tail. Head, neck and throat white with many thin brown streaks; bill hooked downward, grayish with black tip. Wings long and broad, feathers dark brown with paler edges; in flight a large black spot is clearly visible midway on the leading edge of the wing. Tail fan-shaped, white with a single broad black band near tip, occasionally with additional, less distinct, tail bands. Legs covered with brown and white barred feathers, toes yellow. A darker phase, in which the head and entire lower body are brown, is sometimes seen.

Description Female: Nearly identical to male.

Nesting Season: This species is not known to nest in the Adirondacks.

Nest: Not applicable.

Eggs: Not applicable.

Seasonal Status: Typically a winter resident, occasionally observed in other seasons.

Habitat: Open fields and marshes.

Similar Species: The Osprey, *Pandion haliaetus* (Sp, S, F), shares the conspicuous black wing spot of the Rough-legged Hawk, but differs by having a white belly and a less prominent terminal tail band.

Comments: Commonly hovers when hunting.

RED-TAILED HAWK
Buteo jamaicensis
Length: 20-24 inches
Wingspan: 46-54 inches

Variegated brown
Plate 2, No. 1

Description Male: Upper body dark brown, variegated with white, gray and reddish brown. Lower body creamy white with dark brown streaks along sides and typically forming an imperfect breast band. Head pale reddish brown, variegated with dark brown; throat white; bill hooked downward, gray with black tip. Wings long and broad, dark brown, variegated with tan and gray; in flight, a dark hook-shaped marking is clearly visible midway on the leading edge of the wing. Tail fan-shaped, rusty red, white tipped, with a single thin black band near the tip. Legs yellow. A darker, brown-breasted color phase occasionally occurs.

Description Female: Nearly identical to male.

Nesting Season: April.

Nest: Located in trees, typically 35-65 feet above ground, constructed of sticks lined with grasses.

Eggs: Two to four, bluish white to dirty white with many irregular reddish brown markings, 2.3 inches long by 1.8 inches wide.

Seasonal Status: Permanent resident.

Habitat: Highly varied, ranging from woodlands to open fields and along highways.

Similar Species: No other large bird of prey has a conspicuous rusty red tail.

Comments: The easiest of the large hawks to identify because of its conspicuous rusty red tail.

BROAD-WINGED HAWK

Brown

Buteo platypterus

Plate 2, No. 2

Length: 14-17 inches
Wingspan: 34-36 inches

Description Male: Upper body dark brown to grayish brown. Lower body with many thin alternating rusty brown and creamy white bands. Head light brown to grayish brown; throat white; bill hooked downward, dark gray. Wings long and broad, dark brown to grayish brown. Tail fan-shaped, black with thin white tip and two broad white bands. Legs yellow.

Description Female: Nearly identical to male.

Nesting Season: May - June.

Nest: Located in trees, usually 25-40 feet above ground, loosely constructed of sticks and twigs, lined with leaves and feathers.

Eggs: Two to four, dirty white with light brown splotches, 1.95 inches long by 1.58 inches wide.

Seasonal Status: Spring, summer and fall.

Habitat: Dense woodlands.

Similar Species: The Red-shouldered Hawk, *B. lineatus* (Sp, S), has a conspicuous rusty red shoulder patch.

Comments: Migrates in groups called kettles. The smallest Adirondack Buteo. The commonest woodland Buteo.

RED-SHOULDERED HAWK
Buteo lineatus

Reddish brown
Plate 2, No. 3

Length: 17-19 inches
Wingspan: 36-41 inches

Description Male: Upper body feathers dark reddish brown with paler edges. Lower body with many thin alternating rusty brown and creamy white bands. Head pale reddish brown, variegated with dark brown; throat white with some dark brown streaks; bill hooked downward, gray with black tip. Wings long and broad, shoulder area conspicuously rusty red; primary flight feathers black with white bands. Tail fan-shaped, black with four to five narrow white bands. Legs yellow.

Description Female: Nearly identical to male.

Nesting Season: April - May.

Nest: Located in trees, 30-55 feet above ground, loosely constructed of twigs and lined with grasses and feathers.

Eggs: Two to four, bluish white to dirty white with fine light brown markings, 2.2 inches long by 1.7 inches wide.

Seasonal Status: Spring and summer.

Habitat: Woodlands and associated streams.

Similar Species: The Broad-winged Hawk, *Buteo platypterus* (Sp, S, F), is smaller and lacks the red shoulder patch.

Comments: Sometimes feeds on aquatic animals such as crayfish and frogs.

COOPER'S HAWK
Accipiter cooperii

Bluish gray
Plate 2, No. 4

Length: 15-19 inches
Wingspan: 29-34 inches

Description Male: Upper body bluish gray to dark gray. Lower body white, crossed with many thin reddish brown bars. Head: crown blackish gray; sides reddish brown; throat white with many reddish brown streaks; bill hooked downward, gray with black tip. Wings dark bluish gray, displaying many brownish bars on the undersurface during flight. Tail long, rounded, ashy gray, crossed by four to five blackish gray bands. Legs yellowish.

Description Female: Nearly identical to male.

Nesting Season: April - May.

Nest: Located in trees, 20-50 feet above ground, constructed of twigs and lined with leaves and grasses.

Eggs: Three to four, bluish white to greenish white, sometimes with reddish brown spots, 1.95 inches long by 1.48 inches wide.

Seasonal Status: Year-round in the southern region, spring, summer and fall to the north.

Habitat: Open woodlands and orchards.

Similar Species: The Sharp-shinned Hawk, *Accipiter striatus* (Sp, S, F), is slightly smaller, has a squared tail and a grayish crown.

Comments: Usually feeds on songbirds which it captures in flight.

NORTHERN GOSHAWK
Accipiter gentilis

Bluish gray
Plate 3, No. 2

Length: 22-24 inches
Wingspan: 42-45 inches

Description Male: Upper body and wings bluish gray. Lower body white with numerous, thin, dark gray bars. Head mostly black; white stripe over eye; throat white with thin gray streaks; bill hooked downward, bluish gray. Tail long, bluish gray, with 4-5 nearly black bars, and thinly white-tipped. Legs yellow.

Decription Female: Nearly identical to male.

Nesting Season: May.

Nest: Located high in conifer trees, constructed of sticks, lined with strips of bark and grasses.

Eggs: Two to five, bluish white, sometimes with faint yellowish brown spots, 2.32 inches long by 1.75 inches wide.

Seasonal Status: Permanent resident.

Habitat: Mature woodlands.

Similar Species: The Marsh Hawk, *Circus cyaneus* (Sp, S, F), is a resident of marshes and fields. It has pale bluish gray plumage and a conspicuous white rump patch.

Comments: Feeds on other birds, especially Ruffed Grouse. Aggressive defender of its territory.

MARSH HAWK
Circus cyaneus
Length: 19-22 inches
Wingspan: 40-50 inches

Light bluish gray
Plate 3, No. 3

Description Male: Upper body light bluish gray; rump snow white. Lower body: breast gray; belly white, with sparse reddish brown markings. Head light bluish gray; bill hooked downward, dark bluish gray with yellow base. Wings bluish gray with black tips. Tail bluish gray with several darker gray bars, the end bar being widest and darkest. Legs yellow.

Description Female: The gray is replaced with various shades of brown and the throat and lower body are prominently streaked with dark brown.

Nesting Season: May.

Nest: Located on ground in damp meadows or drier fields, usually near water, a loosely constructed platform of grasses and sticks.

Eggs: Four to six, dirty white to bluish white with slightly darker splotches, 1.8 inches long by 1.4 inches wide.

Seasonal Status: Spring, summer and fall.

Habitat: Open areas near marshes and rivers.

Similar Species: The Northern Goshawk, *Accipiter gentilis* (AS), is a woodland resident with darker plumage and white facial markings, and lacks a white rump.

Comments: Also known as a Northern Harrier. Easily identified during flight by its conspicuous white rump patch.

THE FALCONS

GYRFALCON
Falco rusticolus

Bluish gray
Plate 3, No. 4

Length: 20-24 inches
Wingspan: 50-55 inches

Description Male: Upper body bluish gray with numerous darker gray markings. Lower body white, heavily marked with gray chevrons. Head: mostly gray to white with many gray streaks; throat white; bill hooked downward, bluish gray with yellow base. Wings long, pointed, bluish gray with blackish tips. Tail long, bluish gray with several darker gray bars. Legs: upper legs feathered like lower body; feet yellow, bluish gray when young. Both brown and mostly white color phases are known to occur.

Description Female: Nearly identical to male.

Nesting Season: Is not known to nest in the Adirondacks.

Nest: Not applicable.

Eggs: Not applicable.

Season Status: Occasional winter visitant.

Habitat: Fields and rocky slopes.

Similar Species: The Peregrine Falcon, *Falco peregrinus* (AS), is a smaller falcon with darker bluish gray plumage and a black head.

Comments: An Arctic species occasionally driven south during extreme winter weather or a shortage of food. The largest American falcon.

PEREGRINE FALCON
Falco peregrinus

Dark bluish gray
Plate 4, No. 1

Length: 15-20 inches
Wingspan: 40-46 inches

Description Male: Upper body and wings dark bluish gray. Lower body dingy white; belly with many black bars and spots. Head, back of neck and cheek patch beneath the eye black; throat and sides of neck white; bill hooked downward, dark gray with blackish tip. Tail long, bluish gray, with several darker gray bars. Legs: upper legs feathered like lower body; feet yellow.

Description Female: Nearly identical to male.

Nesting Season: March - July.

Nest: A small hollow or scrape located on rocky cliffs. In 1985 Peregrine Falcons successfully nested in the Adirondacks for the first time since the early 1960's. Those now nesting in the Adirondacks are a direct result of the successful restoration program carried out by the New York State Department of Environmental Conservation using captive bred birds from the Peregrine Fund. In 1990, there were nine pairs of peregrine falcons in the Adirondacks, and five of these successfully bred and produced 12 young. It is believed that this number will increase in the future. Locations of known nesting pairs are posted during breeding season.

Eggs: Three to four, creamy white to pale cinnamon brown with irregularly shaped reddish brown markings, 2.1 inches long by 1.65 inches wide.

Seasonal Status: Aside from the newly established resident population, Peregrine Falcons from outside this area are occasional migratory visitants.

Habitat: Open areas and rock cliffs.

Similar Species: The Merlin, *F. columbarius* (Sp, F), is a smaller falcon with similar upper body coloration but lighter cheek patches. The much smaller American Kestrel, *F. sparverius* (AS), has a reddish brown upper body and tail, and a pale gray and brown head.

Comments: An endangered species due to the effect of DDT causing weakness in the eggshell.

AMERICAN KESTREL
Falco sparverius

Reddish brown
Plate 4, No. 3

Length: 10-11 inches
Wingspan: 22-24 inches

Description Male: Upper body reddish brown with large black band-like markings. Lower body pale reddish brown becoming white near rump, with several black spots. Head: top bluish gray with reddish brown spot on crown; sides white with two vertical black bars; back reddish brown with a black spot; throat white; bill hooked downward, dark gray. Wings long and pointed, slate gray with blackish spots and bars. Tail long, reddish brown with broad black band near tip, tip white; outer feathers white usually with black spots. Legs yellow.

Description Female: Similar to male but with reddish brown wings and several dark brown tail bands.

Nesting Season: May.

Nest: Located in tree cavity, usually abandoned Woodpecker or Flicker hole.

Eggs: Four to five, creamy white to tan with many fine chestnut brown specks, 1.36 inches long by 1.12 inches wide.

Seasonal Status: Permanent resident.

Habitat: Fields and other open areas.

Similar Species: The Merlin, *F. columbarius* (Sp, F), a rare migratory visitant, is slightly larger and has a slate gray back, wings and tail. It has three to four dark gray to black tail bars and numerous brown, chevron-like markings on the lower body.

Comments: Also know as a Sparrow Hawk. The smallest Adirondack bird of prey.

THE VULTURES

TURKEY VULTURE Blackish brown
Cathartes aura Plate 4, No. 4
Length: 28-30 inches
Wingspan: 65-72 inches

Description Male: Upper body, lower body and tail blackish brown. Head lacking feathers; skin crimson to cinnamon pink; bill hooked downward, ivory white. Wings blackish brown; primary flight feathers with grayish cast. Legs dull pinkish tan.

Description Female: Nearly identical to male.

Nesting Season: April - May.

Nest: No nest built. Eggs laid in stump hollows or rocky depressions along cliffs.

Eggs: Two, dirty white with dark brown irregular patches, 2.75 inches long by 1.9 inches wide.

Seasonal Status: Spring, summer, fall.

Habitat: Open areas, especially along roadways.

Similar Species: The Black Vulture, *Coragyps atratus* (Sp, S), rarely seen in New York State, surprised ornithologists by appearing in the Adirondacks during the early 1990's. It is a smaller bird with a 55-inch wingspan, a white patch near the tip of each wing and a gray, featherless head.

Comments: This species has a wingspan of six feet. Over the past two decades, Turkey Vultures have become increasingly common in New York State.

Section II
Owls

Great Horned Owl
Bubo virginianus

Owls

Owls are large typically nocturnal meat-eating birds with stout hooked bills and sharp, deeply curved talons. They may be recognized by their unusually large heads, flattened dish-like faces, and large eyes which enable them to see well at night. The eyes are fixed in a forward position, requiring the owl to rotate its head to see in other directions. Size, color, and the presence or absence of horn-like feather tufts are key species identification characteristics.

SNOWY OWL White
Nyctea scandiaca Plate 5, No. 2 & 3
Length: 22-24 inches
Wingspan: 54-59 inches

Description Male: Upper and lower body, top and back of head, wings and tail varying from pure white to white with occasional black to dark brown spots or bars. Face always pure white; eyes yellow; bill stout, curved downward, black. Legs and feet completely covered with white feathers.

Description Female: Similar to male but typically with more black to dark brown markings.

Nesting Season: This bird is not known to nest in the Adirondacks.

Nest: Not applicable.

Eggs: Not applicable.

Seasonal Status: Winter visitant.

Habitat: Open fields and meadows.

Similar Species: No other owl closely resembles this species.

Comments: Hunts during daylight or at night. Typically a resident of Canada and the Arctic Region, it is sometimes driven south by severe winter weather or a shortage of food.

GREAT HORNED OWL
Bubo virginianus

Mottled brown
Plate 5, No. 4

Length: 20-24 inches
Wingspan: 50-60 inches

Description Male: Upper body mottled with yellowish brown, creamy yellow, dark brown and black flecks. Lower body yellowish gray to off-white with numerous fine black bars. Head: top with two prominent horn-like black and brown feather tufts; top and back dark brown with numerous black flecks; face reddish brown to brown with black borders; eyes large, yellow; bill stout, hooked downward, black; often with a white patch below bill. Wings and tail mottled like the upper body, with indistinct brown bars. Legs and feet completely covered with brownish gray feathers.

Description Female: Nearly identical to male.

Nesting Season: February - March.

Nest: Located in abandoned squirrel, crow or hawk nest, sometimes lined with feathers.

Eggs: Two to three, white, 2.26 inches long by 1.87 inches wide.

Seasonal Status: Permanent resident.

Habitat: Mixed woodlands.

Similar Species: The Long-eared Owl, *Asio otus* (AS), is considerably smaller and has both streaks and bars creating a checkered effect on the lower body.

Comments: One of the most commonly observed owls in the Adirondacks. Feeds on a wide variety of prey including ducks, skunks, and mice. Easily recognized by its loud hooting call.

LONG-EARED OWL
Asio otus

Dusky brown
Plate 6, No. 1

Length: 14-16 inches
Wingspan: 38-40 inches

Description Male: Upper body dusky brown, finely mottled with ashy gray and dull orange. Lower body white to cream-white, streaked and barred with brown. Head: top with two prominent horn-like blackish feather tufts; top and back dusky brown with many gray to black flecks; face reddish brown with black borders; eyes large, yellow; area between eyes a mixture of brown and gray; bill stout, curved downward, nearly black. Wings: upper portion dusky brown, finely mottled with ashy gray and dull orange; primary flight feathers ashy brown with yellowish brown bands. Tail ashy brown with yellowish brown bands. Legs and feet completely covered with cream-colored feathers.

Description Female: Nearly identical to male.

Nesting Season: April - May.

Nest: Located in abandoned squirrel, crow or hawk nest, sometimes lined with feathers.

Eggs: Three to six, white, 1.65 inches long by 1.3 inches wide.

Seasonal Status: May be observed year round.

Habitat: Mixed woodlands, prefers to roost in conifers.

Similar Species: The Great Horned Owl, *Bubo virginianus* (AS), is much larger and has bars but no streaks over most of the lower body.

Comments: The frequency of its occurrence within the park is difficult to ascertain due to its similarity to the Great Horned Owl.

SHORT-EARED OWL
Asio flammeus

Yellowish brown
Plate 6, No. 2

Length: 14-16 inches
Wingspan: 40-43 inches

Description Male: Upper body feathers dusky brown with yellow margins. Lower body: breast yellowish brown, heavily streaked with dark brown; belly shading to nearly white, lightly streaked with brown. Head: top with two typically inconspicuous feather tufts; top and back yellowish brown; face nearly round, light brown with a thin nearly white outer border surrounding a thin nearly black inner border; eyes large, yellow, surrounded by small black patches; bill stout, hooked downward, bluish black. Wings mottled with dusky brown, yellow and white. Tail dusky brown with several yellowish brown bands. Legs and feet completely covered with cream-colored feathers.

Description Female: Nearly identical to male.

Nesting Season: April - May.

Nest: Located on the ground in moist areas, constructed of twigs and lined with grasses and some feathers.

Eggs: Three to six, white, 1.55 inches long by 1.25 inches wide.

Seasonal Status: Rare, but may be observed during all seasons.

Habitat: Open meadows and marshes.

Similar Species: The Hawk-Owl, *Surnia ulula* (W), is darker brown, has a longer tail and an almost hawk-like face.

Comments: There has been some speculation that populations of this species are declining across the United States, including the northeast. Sometimes hunts and nests in groups. Occasionally feeds during daylight. One of its calls may be mistaken for the bark of a dog.

HAWK-OWL
Surnia ulula
Length: 15-16 inches
Wingspan: 33-34 inches

Dark brown
Plate 6, No. 3

Description Male: Upper body dark brown to dark grayish brown. Lower body off-white with many thin brown bars. Head: top and back dark brown with many small white spots; face white with black borders; eyes large, yellow; bill stout, hooked downward, yellow. Wings dark brown with cream-white bars. Tail long, rounded, dark brown with cream-white to gray bars. Legs and feet completely covered with grayish brown feathers.

Description Female: Nearly identical to male.

Nesting Season: Is not known to nest in the Adirondacks.

Nest: Not applicable.

Eggs: Not applicable.

Seasonal Status: Rare winter visitant.

Habitat: Clearings near coniferous forests.

Similar Species: The Short-eared Owl, *Asio flammeus* (AS), is lighter brown, has a shorter tail, and a nearly round, typical owl face.

Comments: Our longest tailed owl, sometimes mistaken for a hawk. Known to hunt during day or night. Normally a more northern species but sometimes driven south by severe winter weather or a shortage of food.

GREAT GRAY OWL
Strix nebulosa
Length: 27-29 inches
Wingspan: 54-59 inches

Brownish gray
Plate 6, No. 4

Description Male: Upper body brownish gray mottled with small white markings. Lower body pale gray with brownish streaks on breast. Head: top and back brownish gray; face appearing large, nearly round, gray with a blackish border and numerous concentric dark gray facial rings; eyes small, yellow; bill stout, hooked downward, yellow; with a conspicuous white area below bill. Wings: upper portion brownish gray, primary flight feathers gray with brownish bands. Tail gray with brownish bands. Legs and feet completely covered with light gray feathers.

Description Female: Nearly identical to male.

Nesting Season: Is not known to nest in the Adirondacks.

Nest: Not applicable.

Eggs: Not applicable.

Seasonal Status: Rare winter visitant.

Habitat: Woodlands.

Similar Species: The Barred Owl, *Strix varia* (AS), is much smaller, browner, has a barred breast and brown eyes.

Comments: The largest owl of North America. Typically a resident of boreal forests, occasionally driven south by severe winter weather or a shortage of food.

BARRED OWL
Strix varia
Length: 18-23 inches
Wingspan: 42-48 inches

Grayish brown
Plate 7, No. 1

Description Male: Upper body feathers grayish brown with two or three cream-colored bars. Lower body grayish white to cream; breast covered with brown bars; belly with brown streaks. Head: top and back grayish brown; face nearly round, grayish with a blackish border and several concentric brownish facial rings; eyes dark brown; bill stout, curved downward, yellow. Wings dark brown with paler brown bands. Tail dark brown with dull yellowish brown bands. Legs and feet completely covered with cream-colored feathers.

Description Female: Nearly identical to male.

Nesting Season: April - May.

Nest: Located in hollow tree or deserted crow or hawk nest.

Eggs: Two to four, white, 1.95 inches long by 1.65 inches wide.

Seasonal Status: Permanent resident.

Habitat: Mixed woodlands and wooded swamps.

Similar Species: The Great Gray Owl, *Strix nebulosa* (W), is much larger, grayer, has a streaked breast and yellow eyes.

Comments: Sometimes called the Hoot Owl or Round-headed Owl. The only dark-eyed owl in the Adirondacks. One of the most common owls of this region.

EASTERN SCREECH OWL
Ashy gray
Otus asio
Plate 7, No. 2 & 3

Length: 8.5-9.5 inches
Wingspan: 20-21 inches

Description Male: Gray phase: upper body ashy gray with black streaks and yellowish flecks. Lower body white with black to chestnut brown streaks. Head: top with two conspicuous brownish gray horn-like feather tufts; top and back mixed ashy gray and black; face ashy gray with a black border and several indistinct dark gray concentric facial rings; eyes large, yellow; bill stout, hooked downward, yellowish gray. Wings ashy gray, finely mottled with black, typically with a row of large white spots on the upper portion. Tail ashy gray with darker gray bands. Legs and feet completely covered with grayish feathers. In the rarer red phase, the gray coloration is replaced by bright chestnut red.

Description Female: Nearly identical to male.

Nesting Season: April.

Nest: Located in tree cavity, usually abandoned Woodpecker hole, sometimes thinly lined with feathers.

Eggs: Four to seven, white, 1.4 inches long by 1.2 inches wide.

Seasonal Status: Permanent resident.

Habitat: Woodlands and woodlots.

Similar Species: The Northern Saw-whet Owl, *Aegolius acadicus* (AS), is slightly smaller, has reddish breast streaks, and lacks horn-like feather tufts. The Boreal Owl, *A. funereus* (W), is slightly larger, is dark brown and lacks horn-like feather tufts.

Comments: Also known as the Mottled or Little Horned Owl.

NORTHERN SAW-WHET OWL
Aegolius acadicus

Brown
Cover photo

Length: 7.5-8 inches
Wingspan: 17-18 inches

Description Male: Upper body brown to dark reddish brown with large light brown to white spots. Lower body white; breast and belly heavily marked with thick, reddish brown streaks. Head: top and back dark brown with many tiny white streaks; face nearly round, white at center, becoming brown near margin; eyes large, yellow; bill stout, curved downward, black. Wings dark brown with rows of whitish spots. Tail dark brown with three or four white to tan bars. Legs and feet completely covered with cream to tan feathers.

Description Female: Nearly identical to male.

Nesting Season: March - April.

Nest: Located in tree cavity, usually abandoned Woodpecker hole.

Eggs: Three to six, white, 1.2 inches long by 1 inch wide.

Seasonal Status: Permanent resident.

Habitat: Forests and swampy woodlands.

Similar Species: The Eastern Screech Owl, *Otus asio* (AS), is slightly larger, usually gray, and has horn-like feather tufts. The Boreal Owl, *A. funereus* (W), is larger, darker brown, and has brown, not reddish brown, belly streaks.

Comments: Smallest Adirondack owl. Extremely tolerant of people in close proximity.

BOREAL OWL
Aegolius funereus

Brown
Plate 7, No. 4

Length: 9-10 inches
Wingspan: 22-24 inches

Description Male: Upper body dark brown to slightly reddish brown with large light brown to white spots. Lower body white with thick brown streaks. Head appearing flat-topped; top and back dark brown to almost black, with many tiny white spots; face nearly round, white with a black border; with small dark patches above each eye and below bill; eyes large, yellow; bill stout, curved downward, yellow. Wings dark brown to slightly reddish brown with several rows of large whitish spots. Tail dark brown to slightly reddish brown with several thin grayish white bands. Legs and feet completely covered with whitish feathers.

Description Female: Nearly identical to male.

Nesting Season: This bird is not known to nest in the Adirondacks.

Nest: Not applicable.

Eggs: Not applicable.

Seasonal Status: Rare winter visitant.

Habitat: Mixed woodlands.

Similar Species: The Northern Saw-whet Owl, *A. acadicus* (AS), is smaller, with lighter brown coloration and reddish brown breast streaks. The Eastern Screech Owl, *Otus asio* (AS), is slightly smaller, typically gray, and has horn-like feather tufts.

Comments: Extremely tolerant of people in close proximity. Typically a bird of the boreal forest, sometimes driven south by severe winter weather or a shortage of food.

Section III

Waterfowl

Ring-necked Duck
Aythya collaris

Waterfowl

Waterfowl, as their name implies, are fowl-like birds usually associated with water. They have long necks, broad flat bills, and webbed feet. Waterfowl are usually categorized as swans, geese, or ducks. Swans are by far the largest of the waterfowl and are easily recognized by their pure white plumage and their exceptionally long necks. Geese are midway in size between swans and ducks. They have long necks, proportionately midway in size between those of swans and ducks. Unlike most ducks, males and females have nearly identical coloration. Geese are extremely vocal during migration. Ducks are the smallest waterfowl, having proportionately shorter necks and typically have markedly different plumage between males and females. They are usually divided into two groups, the dabbling ducks and the diving ducks. The dabbling ducks, also known as the pond or puddle ducks, usually feed on the surface, often upending themselves with their head in the water and their tail pointed up. They launch directly into flight from the surface of the water. The diving ducks, sometimes called sea or bay ducks because they are frequently observed along the ocean, feed by diving and swimming under water. Prior to flight, diving ducks run along the surface of the water. In this work, the descriptions from the Wood Duck to the Northern Pintail are dabbling ducks. The descriptions from the Canvasback to the Hooded Merganser are diving ducks.

THE SWANS

TUNDRA SWAN   White
Olor columbianus   Plate 8, No. 1
Length: 52-55 inches
Wingspan: 79-81 inches

Description Male: Large oval body with a very long neck. Entire plumage white. Bill long, flattened, black, sometimes with a yellow spot near the eye. Legs black; toes webbed.

Description Female: Nearly identical to male.

Nesting Season: This species is not known to nest in the Adirondacks.

Nest: Not applicable.

Eggs: Not applicable.

Seasonal Status: Migratory visitant.

Habitat: Rivers, ponds and lakes.

Similar Species: The Mute Swan, *Cygnus olor* (AS), has a yellowish orange bill usually with a large knob at the base. It was introduced from Europe and is sometimes kept as an ornamental.

Comments: Also known as the Whistling Swan and was listed as *Cygnus columbianus*.

THE GEESE

CANADA GOOSE
Branta canadensis
Length: 35-43 inches
Wingspan: 60-66 inches

Grayish brown
Plate 8, No. 3

Description Male: Upper body feathers grayish brown with paler edges. Lower body: breast gray, shading to white on belly. Head black with white cheeks and throat; bill long, flattened, black; neck long, black. Wing feathers grayish brown with paler edges. Tail short, rounded, black. Legs black; toes webbed.

Description Female: Similar to male but slightly paler.

Nesting Season: May - June.

Nest: Located on ground near water, loosely constructed of twigs and grasses, lined with down.

Eggs: Five to ten, dirty white occasionally with pale green tints, 3.5 inches long by 2.5 inches wide.

Seasonal Status: May be observed throughout the year but most common during migratory seasons.

Habitat: Rivers, ponds, lakes and nearby fields.

Similar Species: The Brant, *B. bernicla* (Sp,F), is smaller and has white streaks on the upper neck but lacks the white cheeks of the Canada Goose.

Comments: Frequently observed feeding in cornfields. Commonly seen flying in large V-shaped patterns. Mates for life. Aggressively protects nesting site from predators even as large as a fox.

BRANT   Brownish gray
Branta bernicla   Plate 8, No. 4

Length: 24-26 inches
Wingspan: 48-52 inches

Description Male: Upper body feathers brown with brownish gray margins. Lower body: upper breast black; lower breast ashy gray shading to white on belly. Head black; bill short, flattened, black; neck long, black, with small white markings just below head. Wings: upper portion feathers brown with brownish gray margins; primary flight feathers black. Tail very short, black with white base. Legs black; toes webbed.

Description Female: Nearly identical to male.

Nesting Season: This species is not known to nest in the Adirondacks.

Nest: Not applicable.

Eggs: Not applicable.

Seasonal Status: Migratory visitant.

Habitat: Rivers, ponds and lakes.

Similar Species: The Canada Goose, *B. canadensis* (AS), is larger and has white cheeks but lacks the white upper neck streaks of the Brant.

Comments: The Brant is primarily an ocean bird which nests in northern Greenland and other arctic islands and winters along the Atlantic coast.

SNOW GOOSE

White

Chen caerulescens

Plate 9, No. 1

Length: 27-30 inches
Wingspan: 58-62 inches

Description Male: White phase: upper body, lower body and tail white. Head and neck white, sometimes with slight reddish brown coloration near bill; bill long, flattened, pinkish; neck long. Wings white with black tips. Legs pinkish; toes webbed. Dark phase: upper body dark grayish brown. Lower body any combination of brown and white. Head and neck mostly white. Wings grayish brown, some feathers with conspicuous light gray edges. Tail grayish brown.

Description Female: Nearly identical to male.

Nesting Season: This species is not known to nest in the Adirondacks.

Nest: Not applicable.

Eggs: Not applicable.

Seasonal Status: Migratory visitant.

Habitat: Marshes, ponds and lakes.

Similar Species: The dark phase of the Snow Goose may be mistaken for a Brant, *Branta bernicla* (Sp, F), but the Brant is slightly smaller and has a black head, neck and bill.

Comments: The dark phase is commonly known as the Blue Goose, and was formerly thought to be a separate species. Although the white phase is by far the most common, the percentage of birds exhibiting the dark phase is increasing.

DABBLING DUCKS

WOOD DUCK   Purplish brown
Aix sponsa   Plate 9, No. 2
Length: 17-20 inches
Wingspan: 26-30 inches

Description Male: Upper body dark iridescent and purplish, greenish brown. Lower body: breast reddish chestnut spotted with white; belly white underneath, shading to yellowish gray on sides with conspicuous black and white feathers along the upper margin; breast separated from belly by a prominent black and white crescent. Head with a conspicuous sweeping crest, metallic green with purple iridescence; sides and crest divided by two long, thin, white lines; throat, lower cheek and sides of upper neck white; bill long, flattened, hooked downward at the tip, black with pinkish red base and sides. Wings dark iridescent purple; speculum blue with white border. Tail long, somewhat fan-shaped, dark purple. Legs yellow; toes webbed.

Description Female: A duller grayish brown bird with a conspicuous tear-shaped eye ring.

Nesting Season: May - June.

Nest: Located in hollow tree or stump cavity, constructed of twigs and grasses, lined with down.

Eggs: Eight to fourteen, creamy white, 2.1 inches long by 1.6 inches wide.

Seasonal Status: Spring, summer, fall.

Habitat: Bodies of water surrounded by woodlands.

Similar Species: No Adirondack species closely resembles this bird.

Comments: Wood Ducks have lost a large percentage of their natural nesting sites due to the removal of great numbers of mature trees near water. This loss has been compensated by an intensive program of locating a large number of elevated nesting boxes in prime habitats.

BLACK DUCK Dark brown
Anas rubripes Plate 9, No. 3
Length: 22-24 inches
Wingspan: 33-37 inches

Description Male: Upper body and lower body feathers very dark brown with rusty brown edges. Head: top nearly black; sides, neck and throat light brown heavily lined with thin black streaks; bill long, flattened, dull greenish gray. Wing feathers very dark brown with rusty brown edges; speculum glossy purple-blue bordered by black bands. Tail short, feathers very dark brown with rusty brown edges. Legs dull red to reddish brown; toes webbed.

Decription Female: Nearly identical to male.

Nesting Season: April - May.

Nest: Located on ground among tall vegetation, constructed of weeds and grasses, lined with down.

Eggs: Six to twelve, tan with light olive tints, 2.4 inches long by 1.7 inches wide.

Seasonal Status: Spring, summer, fall.

Habitat: Aquatic areas from marshes and swamps to rivers, ponds and lakes.

Similar Species: The Gadwall, *A. strepera* (Sp, F), is slightly smaller, grayer, has a white belly and a black and white speculum. The Black Duck is nearly identical to the female Mallard, but the Mallard is paler and has both black and white speculum borders.

Comments: Black Ducks have been known to breed with Mallards, producing hybrid offspring exhibiting characteristics of both species. At one time there was speculation that the Black Duck was only a color phase of the closely related Mallard, based partially on the fact that the plumage of an immature Mallard matches that of the described plumage of the adult Black Duck. Some published pictures of young Mallards have been mistakenly identified as being Black Ducks.

MALLARD
Anas platyrhynchos
Length: 22-24 inches
Wingspan: 32-35 inches

Grayish brown with green head
Plate 9, No. 4

Description Male: Upper body dark grayish brown shading to black near tail. Lower body: breast reddish chestnut; belly grayish white, finely marked with thin, wavy black lines. Head and upper neck glossy green, with a white ring on the lower neck; bill long, flattened, yellow with black tip. Wings dark grayish brown; speculum glossy purple-blue bordered by black and white bands. Tail white, four black feathers at base curl upward. Legs orange, toes webbed.

Description Female: Mottled with various shades of brown and cream; speculum glossy purple-blue bordered by black and white bands; bill darker yellow.

Nesting Season: May.

Nest: Located on dry ground near water, well hidden, loosely constructed of grasses and leaves, lined with down.

Eggs: Six to fourteen, tan with light olive tints, 2.3 inches long by 1.6 inches wide.

Seasonal Status: Spring, summer, fall, rare winter visitant.

Habitat: Aquatic areas from marshes and swamps to rivers, ponds and lakes.

Similar Species: The Northern Shoveler, *A. clypeata* (Sp, F), has a white breast, chestnut colored sides and a green speculum.

Comments: One of the best known ducks of the Adirondacks. The ancestor of many farm ducks, such as the Rouen Duck. It superficially resembles the Mallard, but has a stouter body with proportionately smaller wings that lack the ability for prolonged flight.

NORTHERN SHOVELER
Anas clypeata
Length: 18-20 inches
Wingspan: 30-33 inches

Brown with green head
Plate 10, No. 1

Description Male: Upper body brown becoming black near tail. Lower body: breast white; sides and belly reddish chestnut with a white patch near base of tail. Head and neck glossy green; bill very long, wider at tip than base, flattened, nearly black. Wings: upper wing pale blue with green speculum; lower wing brown. Tail short, black with white edges. Legs small, reddish; toes webbed.

Description Female: Mottled with various shades of brown and cream; speculum green; forewing blue.

Nesting Season: This species is not known to nest in the Adirondacks.

Nest: Not applicable.

Eggs: Not applicable.

Seasonal Status: Migratory visitant.

Habitat: Rivers, ponds and lakes.

Similar Species: The Mallard, *A. platyrhynchos* (AS), has a chestnut colored breast, grayish white sides and a blue speculum.

Comments: Also known as the Spoonbill.

BLUE-WINGED TEAL　　　　Brown with gray head
Anas discors　　　　　　　　　Plate 10, No. 2
Length: 15-16 inches
Wingspan: 27-30 inches

Description Male: Upper body variegated dark brown and yellowish brown, shading to dark greenish brown near the tail. Lower body pale cinnamon brown with numerous small black spots, with a white patch near base of tail. Head: crown dark brown to black; sides and neck purplish lead gray, with a conspicuous crescent-shaped white patch in front of each eye; bill long, flattened, grayish black. Wings: upper wing pale blue with green speculum; lower wing brown. Tail short, dark brown. Legs dark yellow; toes webbed.

Description Female: Mottled with various shades of brown and cream; speculum green; forewing blue.

Nesting Season: May - June.

Nest: Located on ground among tall vegetation near water, constructed of grasses and weeds, lined with feathers and down.

Eggs: Six to twelve, tan, sometimes with olive tints, 1.85 inches long by 1.3 inches wide.

Seasonal Status: Spring, summer, fall.

Habitat: Marshes and ponds.

Similar Species: No other Adirondack duck closely resembles this species.

Comments: Can fly nearly fifty miles per hour for limited distances.

———————————————

GREEN-WINGED TEAL
Anas crecca
Length: 14 inches
Wingspan: 23 inches

Gray with chestnut head
Plate 10, No. 3

Description Male: Upper body gray with many thin black bars, becoming grayish brown near tail. Lower body: upper breast pale yellowish brown with many small black spots; lower breast and belly whitish; sides with many thin black bars and a white crescent-shaped patch below each shoulder, with a creamy yellow patch near base of tail. Head slightly crested; head and neck reddish chestnut; area from eye to back of head glossy green; bill long, flattened, black. Wings dull gray; speculum half glossy green and half glossy purple with white border. Tail short, grayish. Legs grayish yellow; toes webbed.

Description Female: Mottled with various shades of brown and cream; speculum green.

Nesting Season: May - June.

Nest: Located on ground among tall vegetation near water, constructed of grasses and weeds, lined with feathers and down.

Eggs: Six to twelve, tan, sometimes with olive tints, 1.8 inches long, 1.3 inches wide.

Seasonal Status: Spring, summer, fall.

Habitat: Swamps, rivers and ponds.

Similar Species: The American Wigeon, *A. americana* (Sp, F), also has a green eye patch, but is larger, has pale pinkish purple body tints and a white crown.

Comments: This bird typically breeds in Canada and only occasionally nests in the Adirondacks. It often feeds at night. The smallest of the puddle ducks.

AMERICAN WIGEON
Anas americana
Length: 19-20 inches
Wingspan: 31-34 inches

Grayish brown
Plate 10, No. 4

Description Male: Upper body grayish brown with pale pinkish purple tints. Lower body: upper breast and sides light reddish brown; belly white. Head: forehead and crown white, with a glossy blackish green patch enclosing the eye and back of head; remaining portions of head and neck yellowish gray, heavily speckled with black; bill long, flattened, grayish blue with black tip. Wings: primary flight feathers brown; speculum glossy green with black borders; white patch above speculum; longer feathers near body black with pale gray edges. Tail short, feathers nearly black with gray edges. Legs dark brown; toes webbed.

Description Female: Similar to male but lacks white crown and blackish green eye patch.

Nesting Season: This species is not known to nest in the Adirondacks.

Nest: Not applicable.

Eggs: Not applicable.

Seasonal Status: Migratory visitant.

Habitat: Marshes, lakes and ponds.

Similar Species: The Green-winged Teal, *A. crecca* (Sp, S, F), also has a green eye patch, but is smaller, grayer, and has chestnut brown head coloration.

Comment: Because of the male's white crown, this bird has been called the Bald Pate.

NORTHERN PINTAIL
Anas acuta

Gray with brown head
Plate 11, No. 1

Length: 25-30 inches
Wingspan: 34-36 inches

Description Male: Upper body gray, heavily marked with many narrow, wavy, black bars. Lower body white; sides heavily marked with many narrow wavy black bars. Head, throat and back of neck olive brown with a single vertical white stripe on each side; front and sides of neck white; bill long, flattened, slate gray. Wings gray; speculum glossy bronze with greenish tints, with white outer border and cinnamon brown inner border. Feathers near body black with white margins. Tail extremely long, slender and pointed, black with gray margins. Legs slate gray; toes webbed.

Description Female: Upper body, lower body, wings and tail mottled with yellowish brown and dark brown. Head and neck pale brown with dark brown flecks. Tail pointed, but shorter than male.

Nesting Season: This species is not known to nest in the Adirondacks.

Nest: Not applicable.

Eggs: Not applicable.

Seasonal Status: Migratory visitant.

Habitat: Marshes, lakes and ponds.

Similar Species: The Oldsquaw, *Clangula hyemalis* (Sp, F), an occasional migratory visitant, also has a long pointed tail, but has a brown breast.

Comments: Also known as Pintail and Common Pintail.

DIVING DUCKS

CANVASBACK Pale gray with chestnut brown head
Aythya valisineria Plate 11, No. 2
Length: 20-22 inches
Wingspan: 33-35 inches

Description Male: Upper body silvery gray with many fine wavy black bands; areas near head and tail black. Lower body: breast black; belly white; sides grayish white. Head and neck chestnut brown to dark reddish brown; crown nearly black; eye red; bill unusually long, flattened, dark bluish gray to nearly black. Wings pale gray with brownish primary flight feathers. Tail short, pointed, slate gray. Legs bluish gray; toes webbed.

Description Female: Upper and lower body and wings brownish slate gray. Head, neck and breast pale wood brown; eye dark brown.

Nesting Season: This species is not known to nest in the Adirondacks.

Nest: Not applicable.

Eggs: Not applicable.

Seasonal Status: Migratory visitant.

Habitat: Marshes and lakes.

Similar Species: The Redhead, *A. americana* (Sp, F), is a bit smaller, has a shorter bluish gray bill with a black tip and yellowish orange eyes.

Comments: Flies in V-formations like Canadian geese.

REDHEAD   Gray with a chestnut brown head
Aythya americana   Plate 11, No. 3
Length: 19-21 inches
Wingspan: 32-33 inches

Description Male: Upper body silvery gray with many wavy black bands; areas near head and tail black. Lower body: breast black; belly white; sides grayish white. Head and neck chestnut brown to dark reddish brown; eye yellowish orange; bill long, flattened, dull bluish gray with black tip. Wings brownish gray with minute white flecks; speculum ashy gray with black borders. Tail short, grayish brown. Legs grayish brown; toes webbed.

Description Female: Dark grayish brown overall; bill dull bluish gray with black tip.

Nesting Season: This species is not known to nest in the Adirondacks.

Nest: Not applicable.

Eggs: Not applicable.

Seasonal Status: Migratory visitant.

Habitat: Marshes, ponds and lakes.

Similar Species: The Canvasback. *A. valisineria* (Sp, F), is slightly larger, has a longer blackish bill and red eyes.

Comments: Prefers to feed at night. The population level of this species has been declining over the past several decades.

RING-NECKED DUCK   Black and gray
Aythya collaris   Plate 11, No. 4

Length: 17 inches
Wingspan: 30 inches

Description Male: Upper body black. Lower body: breast black; sides gray; belly white; a white crescent separates the breast from the sides. Head and neck dark glossy purple; lower neck with an inconspicuous reddish brown ring; eye orange; bill long, flattened, very broad, nearly black with a white ring near the tip and a white base. Wings black with dark brown primary flight feathers and a gray speculum. Tail short, dark brown. Legs slate gray; toes webbed.

Description Female: Plumage mottled brown overall; eye dark brown; white eye ring and eye bar; white ring near tip of bill.

Nesting Season: May - June.

Nest: Located on ground near water, constructed of grasses, lined with feathers.

Eggs: Six to twelve, grayish tan sometimes with olive tints, 2.25 inches long by 1.6 inches wide.

Seasonal Status: Spring, summer, fall.

Habitat: Marshes, ponds and lakes.

Similar Species: The Lesser Scaup, *A. affinis* (Sp, F), has a gray upper body, a white speculum, yellowish eyes and a bluish gray bill with a black tip. The Greater Scaup, *A. marila* (Sp, F), is nearly identical to the Lesser Scaup, but has a glossy dark green head and neck. Neither Scaup has a neck or bill ring.

Comments: Also known as the Ring-billed Duck and Ring-necked Scaup.

COMMON GOLDENEYE
Bucephala clangula
Length: 17-20 inches
Wingspan: 24-30 inches

Black and white
Plate 12, No. 1

Description Male: Upper body black with white streaking near wings. Lower body white. Head and upper neck black with a greenish iridescence and a round white spot between the bill and eye; eye golden yellow; lower neck white; bill short, flattened, black. Wings black with white speculum. Tail short, black. Legs orangish; toes webbed.

Description Female: Upper body and sides brownish gray; head brown with a white neck ring.

Nesting Season: May - June.

Nest: Located in a hollow tree or stump, constructed of leaves and mosses, lined with down.

Eggs: Six to twelve, bright green to grayish green, 2.4 inches long by 1.7 inches wide.

Seasonal Status: Permanent resident.

Habitat: Rivers and lakes.

Similar Species: Barrow's Goldeneye, *B. islandica* (Sp, F), a rare visitant, is larger, has a purplish iridescence on the head, a crescent-shaped white patch between the eye and bill and a series of white oval patches along the sides of the body. The Bufflehead, *B. albeola* (Sp, F), is smaller, has a white fan-shaped patch covering the sides and back of the head, and has nearly black eyes.

Comments: Also known as the Whistler because its rapid flight is accompanied by a sharp whistling sound.

BUFFLEHEAD Black and white
Bucephala albeola Plate 12, No. 3
Length: 14-15 inches
Wingspan: 23-25 inches

Description Male: Upper body black with purplish green iridescence. Lower body white. Head and throat black with a purplish green iridescence; white fan-shaped patch on sides and back of head; lower neck white; eyes nearly black; bill short, flattened, dull blue. Wings black; speculum and forewing patch white. Tail short, gray. Legs pinkish brown; toes webbed.

Description Female: Upper body, wings and tail brown; sides grayish brown; head dark brown with small white facial patch.

Nesting Season: This species in not known to nest in the Adirondacks.

Nest: Not applicable.

Eggs: Not applicable.

Seasonal Status: Migratory visitant.

Habitat: Rivers and lakes.

Similar Species: The Common Goldeneye, *B. clangula* (AS), is larger, has a round white patch between the eye and the bill, and has golden yellow eyes.

Comments: Also known as the Butter-ball and Little Dipper.

COMMON EIDER
Somateria mollissima
Length: 23-26 inches
Wingspan: 34-40 inches

Black and white
Plate 12, No. 4

Description Male: Upper body: upper back white; lower back black. Lower body: breast white with faint peach-colored tints; belly and sides black. Head: crown black with a thin central white stripe; sides and neck white with greenish tinges on sides and back of neck; bill long, flattened, extending onto forehead, pale olive gray. Wings black with large white upper wing patches. Tail pointed, black. Legs dull olive green; toes webbed.

Description Female: Mottled brown overall with a black speculum and grayish bill.

Nesting Season: This species in not known to nest in the Adirondacks.

Nest: Not applicable.

Eggs: Not applicable.

Seasonal Status: Migratory visitant.

Habitat: Rivers and lakes.

Similar Species: No other Adirondack duck closely resembles this species.

Comments: Usually nests on the northern shores of Canada.

RUDDY DUCK
Oxyura jamaicensis

Reddish brown
Plate 13, No. 1

Length: 15-16 inches
Wingspan: 20-24 inches

Description Male: Upper body rusty reddish brown. Lower body: breast and sides rusty reddish brown; belly white. Head: crown and back black; sides and throat white; lower neck rusty reddish brown; bill long, flattened, broadest at tip, pale blue. Wings dark reddish brown. Tail often borne erect, dark brown. Legs brownish; toes webbed.

Description Female: Upper body and crown brownish gray to dark brown. Lower body grayish white with many thin blackish bars. Bill dark gray.

Nesting Season: This species is not known to nest in the Adirondacks.

Nest: Not applicable.

Eggs: Not applicable.

Seasonal Status: Migratory visitant.

Habitat: Marshes, ponds, rivers and lakes.

Similar Species: No other Adirondack duck closely resembles this species.

Comments: Also known as the Stiff-tailed Wigeon, Bluebill, and Broad-bill Dipper.

HOODED MERGANSER
Lophodytes cucullatus

Black and white
Plate 13, No. 2

Length: 17-19 inches
Wingspan: 25-28 inches

Description Male: Upper body black becoming brownish near tail. Lower body: breast white with two crescent-shaped black bands; belly cream-white with reddish brown sides. Head with large fan-shaped crest, black with large white patch on both sides of crest; bill long, cylindrical, serrated, with a downward hooked tip, bluish black. Wings black with white markings. Tail dark brown to nearly black. Legs black; toes webbed.

Description Female: The male's black plumage is replaced with various shades of brown. The crest is much smaller, rusty brown and lacks the distinctive white patches.

Nesting Season: May - June.

Nest: Located in tree or stump cavity, lined with grasses, leaves and down.

Eggs: Five to fifteen, ivory white, 2.1 inches long by 1.75 inches wide.

Seasonal Status: Spring, summer and fall.

Habitat: Bodies of water bordered by woodlands.

Similar Species: The Common Merganser, *Mergus merganser* (AS), which also breeds in the Adirondacks, is much larger, has a red bill and an iridescent green head which lacks a crest. The Red-breasted Merganser, *M. serrator* (Sp, F), is slightly smaller than the Common Merganser. It closely resembles the Common Merganser, but has a crested head and reddish brown breast plumage.

Comments: Frequently competes with Wood Ducks for nesting sites. Smallest of the mergansers found in the Adirondacks.

Section IV
Shore and Water Birds

Common Loon
Gavia immer

Shore and Water Birds

This is a large and diverse section which includes most birds associated with water but excludes swans, geese and ducks. We have arranged the section into the following groups: deep water swimmers, gulls and terns, the ibis, herons, swimming shore birds, and the rail, plover, and sandpiper group. The deep water swimmers are the Loon and Double-crested Cormorant. Both are long-necked and web-footed birds found on large bodies of water. Gulls and terns are well-known long-winged, web-footed birds associated with large bodies of water. Gulls are larger birds with stouter bodies and short, fan-shaped tails; terns are smaller, sleeker birds with long forked tails. The Glossy Ibis, a recent newcomer to the Adirondack waterways, is a wading bird with long legs, a long neck and an exceptionally long, down-curved bill. Members of the heron family are also wading birds, with long legs and long, straight bills. This group includes the white egrets, several heron species and the bitterns. The swimming shore birds, the Common Moorhen, the American Coot, and the grebes, may be differentiated from the ducks by their chicken-like bodies, shorter pointed bills, and non or incompletely webbed feet. The rail, plover and sandpiper group is an artificial group which we use here to include the smaller, long-legged wading birds which usually feed in marshes and along shorelines. This group also includes two species that frequent meadows and fields far from water, the Killdeer and the Upland Sandpiper.

THE DEEP WATER SWIMMERS

COMMON LOON   Black and white
Gavia immer   Plate 13, No. 3
Length: 28-35 length
Wingspan: 48-52 inches

Description Male: Upper body glossy black with many rows of square, white markings. Lower body white with short black streaks along sides. Head black with slight green iridescence; throat black with large black and white band encircling most of the neck and a small black and white patch on the throat slightly above this band; eye red; bill stout, straight, sharply pointed, dark gray. Wings black with numerous rows of white spots. Tail short, black. Legs short, black; feet webbed.

Description Female: Nearly identical to male.

Nesting Season: May - June

Nest: Located on the ground near water, constructed of reeds, rushes and other aquatic plants.

Eggs: Two, olive brown, 3.25 inches long by 2.1 inches wide.

Seasonal Status: Spring, summer and fall.

Habitat: Remote lakes and large ponds.

Similar Species: The Double-crested Cormorant, *Phalacrocorax auritus* (Sp, F), has a hooked bill, a longer tail and solid black coloration.

Comments: Previously known as the Northern Diver. Dives to depths well over 200 feet. The loon, a symbol of the Adirondack wilderness, is known for its mournful cry.

DOUBLE-CRESTED CORMORANT
Phalacrocorax auritus
Length: 30-32 inches
Wingspan: 46-48 inches

Black
Plate 13, No. 4

Description Male: Upper body glossy iridescent black. Lower body black. Head black with two short feather tufts on crown; neck long and black; throat dull orange to orange-red; eye turquoise green; bill long, hooked downward; upper mandible dark gray; lower mandible dark gray with dull orange base. Wings black. Tail long, rounded, black. Legs dark gray; toes webbed.

Description Female: Nearly identical to male.

Nesting Season: This species in not known to nest in the Adirondacks.

Nest: Not applicable.

Eggs: Not applicable.

Seasonal Status: Migratory visitant.

Habitat: Rivers and lakes.

Similar Species: The Common Loon, *Gavia immer* (Sp, S, F), has a straight bill, a short tail and is black with many white markings.

Comments: Highly skilled at fishing.

GULLS AND TERNS

RING-BILLED GULL
Larus delawarensis
Length: 18-20 inches
Wingspan: 49 inches

Gray and white
Plate 14, No. 1

Description Male: Upper body: area between wings pearl gray; upper shoulders and rump white. Lower body white. Head white; bill slightly hooked downward, yellow with black ring near tip. Wings pearl gray, tips black with some white markings. Tail white. Legs pale yellow to greenish yellow.

Description Female: Nearly identical to male.

Nesting Season: May.

Nest: Located on ground in a small hollow, lined with grasses.

Eggs: Two to three, pale brown with chocolate brown markings, 2.4 inches long by 1.7 inches wide.

Seasonal Status: Spring, summer and fall.

Habitat: Rivers, ponds and lakes, frequently feeding at dumps and landfills.

Similar Species: The Herring Gull, *L. argentatus* (AS), is a larger bird with pinkish legs, lacks the black bill ring but has a reddish patch near the tip of the lower mandible. Terns may be differentiated from gulls by their smaller, more streamlined bodies, forked tails and straight, pointed bills.

Comments: Within the Adirondacks, the Ring-billed Gull commonly nests only in the Lake Champlain Region. The reddish bill patch of the Herring Gull is struck by its young as a signal for feeding.

COMMON TERN
Sterna hirundo

Gray and white
Plate 15, No. 2

Length: 14-15 inches
Wingspan: 30-31 inches

Description Male: Upper body pearl gray with white rump. Lower body grayish shading to white on belly. Head: cap and back of neck black; sides and throat white; bill long, sharp, coral red with black tip. Wings pearl gray shading to dark gray near tips. Tail long, forked, white with grayish edges. Legs light reddish orange.

Description Female: Nearly identical to male.

Nesting Season: This species is not known to nest in the Adirondacks.

Nest: Not applicable.

Eggs: Not applicable.

Seasonal Status: Migratory visitant.

Habitat: Along marhses, ponds and lakes.

Similar Species: The Black Tern, *Chlidonias niger* (Sp, S, F), has a black head and lower body and dark gray upper body, wings and tail. Gulls may be differentiated from terns by their larger size, stouter body, squared tail and slightly hooked bill.

Comments: Feeds by skimming over water searching for aquatic insects and minnows.

THE IBIS

GLOSSY IBIS
Plegadis falcinellus
Length: 22-24 inches
Wingspan: 35-36 inches

Dark reddish brown
Plate 15, No. 4

Description Male: Upper and lower body dark reddish brown. Head dark reddish brown; bill very long, slightly curved downward, dark gray; neck long, slender, dark reddish brown. Wings iridescent dark green. Tail very short, dark reddish brown. Legs very long, dark gray.

Description Female: Nearly identical to male.

Nesting Season: This species is not known to nest in the Adirondacks.

Nest: Not applicable.

Eggs: Not applicable.

Seasonal Status: Rare summer visitant.

Habitat: Marshes, rivers and lakes.

Similar Species: No other Adirondack bird closely resembles this species.

Comments: Appears nearly black at a distance. Previously a southern shorebird, this species has been rapidly expanding its range northward, and now breeds regularly in southeastern New York.

THE HERONS

CATTLE EGRET   White
Bubulcus ibis   Plate 16, No. 1

Length: 18-20 inches
Wingspan: 28-34.5 inches

Description Male: Upper body, lower body, head, wings and tail white. Bill long, straight, yellow. Legs long, dark yellow. When breeding, the crown, breast and lower back become pale brown to pale orange, the bill and legs become more orange.

Description Female: Nearly identical to male.

Nesting Season: June.

Nest: Located in low trees or bushes near water, constructed of sticks and branches.

Eggs: Four to six, pale blue, 1.5 inches long by 1.2 inches wide.

Seasonal Status: Spring, summer and fall.

Habitat: Along rivers and lakes.

Similar Species: The Great Egret, *Casmerodius albus* (S), a rare summer visitant, is a much larger bird, 35-40 inches long with black legs.

Comments: The Cattle Egret, native to Africa, first arrived in America in the 1950's. It has been steadily expanding its range in the United States and populations in the Adirondacks are likely to increase.

GREAT BLUE HERON   Ashy blue
Ardea herodias   Plate 16, No. 3
Length: 42-50 inches
Wingspan: 68-74 inches

Description Male: Upper body ashy to slate gray. Lower body grayish white. Head: sides white; crest long, black, with white crown; area around eye blue and lacking feathers; neck exceptionally long and slender, light brownish; throat white, edged with black feathers; bill long, sharp, mostly yellow, black on uppermost surface. Wings dark ashy blue with black shoulders. Tail short, ashy blue to slate gray. Legs very long, dark gray to black, feathers on upper portion rusty brown. During mating season, breast and back covered with long, loose, bluish gray feathers.

Description Female: Nearly identical to male.

Nesting Season: May.

Nest: Located high in trees, loosely constructed of twigs and branches, usually as part of a colony.

Eggs: Three to four, dull greenish blue, 2.5 inches long by 1.5 inches wide.

Seasonal Status: Spring, summer and fall.

Habitat: Creeks, rivers, ponds and lakes.

Similar Species: The Little Blue Heron, *Egretta caerulea* (Sp, S, F), very rare in the Adirondacks, is only half as large, has an ashy blue body and wings, a brown tinted head and neck, and a black-tipped grayish bill.

Comments: Feeds by capturing fish in shallow water. The tallest bird in the Adirondacks.

BLACK-CROWNED NIGHT-HERON   Black and gray
Nycticorax nycticorax   Plate 17, No. 1 & 2
Length: 23-26 inches
Wingspan: 43-46 inches

Description Male: Upper body black to greenish black. Lower body white. Head disproportionately large: side, forehead and throat white; top and back of head black to greenish black, with two or three 6 to 8-inch white feathers extending from the back of the head; eye red; area around eye featherless and blue; bill stout, pointed, black. Wings ashy gray. Tail very short, ashy gray. Legs yellow.

Description Female: Nearly identical to male.

Nesting Season: May - June.

Nest: Located high up in trees, usually as part of a colony, loosely constructed of large twigs and branches.

Eggs: Four to six, pale bluish green, 2 inches long by 1.5 inches wide.

Seasonal Status: Spring, summer and fall.

Habitat: Along lakes and marshes.

Similar Species: The Yellow-crowned Night-Heron, *N. violaceus* (Sp, S, F), is a rare visitant. It has a gray upper body and wings, and a black head with a white crown and white cheek patches. The Green-backed Heron, *Butorides striatus* (Sp, S, F), is a smaller bird with dark green wings and a chestnut brown neck.

Comments: Also known as Quawk, a name patterned after its hoarse cry. Often vocal at night.

GREEN-BACKED HERON
Butorides striatus

Green and brown
Plate 17, No. 4

Length: 16-18 inches
Wingspan: 24-25 inches

Description Male: Upper body dark glossy green. Lower body ashy white. Head: sides of head and sides of neck chestnut brown; top crested and dark green; eye and eye bar yellow; throat white with dark brown edging; bill stout and sharp; upper mandible black; lower mandible yellow. Wings dark green with bluish tinge, many feathers with narrow white edging. Tail short, dark green. Legs yellow to greenish yellow.

Description Female: Nearly identical to male.

Nesting Season: June.

Nest: Located in trees, a loosely constructed platform of sticks and twigs.

Eggs: Three to six, dull blue to pale green, 1.5 inches long by 1.15 inches wide.

Seasonal Status: Spring, summer and fall.

Habitat: Along lakes and marshes.

Similar Species: The Black-crowned Night-Heron, *Nycticorax nycticorax* (Sp, S, F), is a larger bird with ashy gray wings and neck, white face and two or three exceptionally long white feathers extending from the back of the head.

Comments: Also known as the Green Heron.

AMERICAN BITTERN
Botaurus lentiginosus

Brown
Plate 18, No. 1

Length: 23-34 inches
Wingspan: 32-45 inches

Description Male: Upper body heavily variegated, a mixture of dark brown to yellow-brown. Lower body creamy white with long brown streaks. Head and back of neck light brown, with a thin creamy white streak above eye; side of neck glossy black; throat white with brown streaks; bill long, straight, yellow with black edges. Wings brown to yellow-brown, with black tips. Tail short, rounded, brown to yellow-brown. Legs long, olive yellow.

Description Female: Nearly identical to male.

Nesting Season: May - June.

Nest: Located on the ground in marshes, a platform constructed of reeds.

Eggs: Three to six, drab brown with olive tints, 1.9 inches long by 1.45 inches wide.

Seasonal Status: Spring, summer and fall.

Habitat: Bogs and marshes.

Similar Species: The Least Bittern, *Ixobrychus exilis* (Sp, S, F), is a much smaller bird, only 11-13 inches long, with black crown, upper body and tail, and a large yellowish brown wing patch. This bird is very rare in the Adirondacks.

Comments: When approached, the American Bittern freezes and points its bill upward. In this position the Bittern is nearly indistinguishable from surrounding reeds.

RAILS, PLOVERS AND SANDPIPERS

VIRGINIA RAIL   Brown
Rallus limicola   Plate 18, No. 2
Length: 9.5-10.5 inches
Wingspan: 13.5-14 inches

Description Male: Upper body brown with black streaks. Lower body: breast yellowish brown to cinnamon brown; belly with black and white bars. Head: crown dark brown; sides gray; black and white bars between eyes and bill; throat white; bill very long, slightly curved downward, dull red with darker tip. Wings reddish brown. Tail very short, pointed upward, dark brown. Legs very long, pinkish orange.

Description Female: Nearly identical to male.

Nesting Season: May - June.

Nest: Located on a grassy platform among sedges and reeds near water.

Eggs: Six to twelve, cream-colored with sparse brown or lavender spots, 1.25 inches long by 0.9 inch wide.

Seasonal Status: Spring, summer and fall.

Habitat: Marshes and swamps.

Similar Species: The Sora, *Porzana carolina* (Sp, S, F), is slightly smaller, has a black throat, a short stout yellow bill and greenish legs. Although we are unable to confirm its presence, the King Rail, *R. elegans* (Sp, S, F), is believed by some to visit the Adirondack Park. It is nearly identical to the Virginia Rail, but twice as large.

Comments: Rails have a chicken-like body. Due to their secretive lifestyle, they are seldom observed.

COMMON MOORHEN
Gallinula chloropus
Length: 12-13 inches
Wingspan: 20-22 inches

Brown and slate gray
Plate 18, No. 4

Description Male: Upper body brown to grayish brown. Lower body slate gray. Head and neck slate gray; bill short, stout, extending over forehead, orange to reddish orange with yellow tip. Wings brown with white feathers along lower edge. Tail short, brown with white feathers along sides. Legs long; feet disproportionately large, pale green.

Description Female: Nearly identical to male.

Nesting Season: May - June.

Nest: Located on the ground in marshes, constructed of reeds and rushes.

Eggs: Seven to thirteen, pale creamy brown with darker brown specks, 1.8 inches long by 1.2 inches wide.

Seasonal Status: Spring, summer and fall.

Habitat: Marshes, rivers, ponds and lakes.

Similar Species: The American Coot, *Fulica americana* (Sp, F), is slightly larger, is slate gray overall and has an ivory white bill.

Comments: Has been described as a chicken on stilts. Also known as the Common Gallinule.

Section V
Upland Game Birds

Ruffed Grouse
Bonasa umbellus

Upland Game Birds

This is a diverse group of species that have traditionally been considered game birds of upland fields and woodlands. It should be noted that some of these birds, such as the Mourning Dove, Spruce Grouse, and Wild Turkey, are protected by the New York State Department of Environmental Conservation. Other members of this group include the American Woodcock, Common Snipe, Ring-necked Pheasant, Ruffed Grouse, and Rock Dove.

AMERICAN WOODCOCK
Scolopax minor
Length: 10-12 inches
Wingspan: 17-19 inches

Variegated brown
Plate 21, No. 1

Description Male: Upper body variegated, a mixture of gray, black, brown and tan. Lower body tan to light brown. Head tan to light brown; back black with three tan bars; an indistinct black eye bar; bill much longer than head, pale brown. Wings pale brown to brown with grayish bands. Tail very short, black with white tip. Legs very short, brown.

Description Female: Nearly identical to male.

Nesting Season: May.

Nest: Located on ground in a shallow depression, lined with leaves.

Eggs: Four, cream-colored with many pale reddish brown spots, 1.55 inches long, by 1.15 inches wide.

Seasonal Status: Spring, summer and fall.

Habitat: Swamps and bogs, moist fields and woodlands.

Similar Species: The Common Snipe, *Gallinago gallinago* (Sp, S, F), has longer legs, a white belly, longer wings and a distinctly reddish orange tail.

Comments: The long bill is used to probe for worms in wet meadows and other soft soils.

WILD TURKEY   Copper brown
Meleagris gallopavo   Plate 21, No. 3
Length: 46-49 inches
Wingspan: 48-56 inches

Description Male: Upper body feathers brown with copper sheen and black tips. Lower body feathers brown with bronze to greenish sheen; a "beard" of hair-like feathers hangs from the center of the breast. Head and upper neck lack feathers; skin bluish gray to bright red; wattles red, becoming especially conspicuous during mating season; bill light brown. Wings brown with a bronze sheen, primary feathers with many whitish bars. Tail feathers reddish brown with many, thin, dark brown bars, tip reddish brown with a wide dark brown band above. Legs dull pinkish red, with a prominent spur.

Description Female: Smaller, with a mostly bluish gray head and no breast beard.

Nesting Season: May - June.

Nest: Located on the ground in woodlands, consisting of a small hollow, lined with leaves and grasses.

Eggs: Nine to fifteen, pale yellow with small brown spots, 2.55 inches long by 1.8 inches wide.

Seasonal Status: Permanent resident.

Habitat: Woodlands and adjoining fields.

Similar Species: The Domestic Turkey has white-tipped tail and chest feathers.

Comments: Although once extirpated from the Adirondacks, the Wild Turkey is beginning to reappear as a result of a restocking effort. During mating displays, the male may open his tail like a fan. Male maintains a harem of 4 to 15 hens.

RING-NECKED PHEASANT
Phasianus colchicus
Length: 32-36 inches
Wingspan: 32 inches

Variegated brown
with green head
Plate 21, No. 4

Description Male: Upper body: upper back light brown to reddish brown with numerous black and white markings; lower back grayish brown to greenish brown with black markings. Lower body feathers glossy copper brown with black tips; sides yellow-brown with black tips. Head green with purplish iridescence; wattles around eyes scarlet red, lacking feathers; white ring encircling base of neck; bill dingy yellow. Wings various shades of brown and gray with numerous black and white markings. Tail very long, pointed, light brown with narrow black bars running the entire length. Legs dull gray.

Description Female: Has a shorter tail and dull brown coloration overall.

Nesting Season: May - June.

Nest: Located on the ground in fields and hedgerows, constructed of grasses.

Eggs: Eight to fifteen, brown with olive tints, 1.6 inches long by 1.3 inches wide.

Seasonal Status: Permanent resident.

Habitat: Fields, hedgerows and agricultural areas.

Similar Species: The Green Pheasant, a color variant of the Ring-necked Pheasant, was occasionally released but is not known to have reproduced in the wild. It differs by having a metallic green lower body and lacks the white neck ring.

Comments: Originally a Chinese bird. Introduced from foreign stock. Rare in the Adirondacks.

RUFFED GROUSE
Bonasa umbellus
Length: 16-18 inches
Wingspan: 23-24 inches

Grayish brown
Plate 22, No. 2

Description Male: Upper body grayish brown to reddish brown, heavily mottled with dull yellow, gray and black. Lower body tan to dull white with numerous pale brown bars. Head crested, brown with tan markings; white eye bar; throat tan; large ruffs of black feathers on sides of neck; bill grayish brown. Wings grayish brown to reddish brown, heavily mottled with dull yellow, gray and black. Tail broad, grayish brown to reddish brown, with numerous thin black and tan bars and a broad blackish band near tip. Legs gray.

Description Female: Similar to male, but lacking conspicuous black neck ruff.

Nesting Season: May.

Nest: Located on ground in woodlands in a shallow depression, lined with leaves, often at base of a tree or under a bush.

Eggs: Eight to fourteen, cream-white, sometimes slightly brown speckled, 1.56 inches long by 1.13 inches wide.

Seasonal Status: Permanent resident.

Habitat: Mixed woodlands.

Similar Species: The Spruce Grouse, *Dendragapus canadensis* (AS), has a black face, throat and breast, a patch of red skin over the eyes and a broad, nearly black, orange-tipped tail. This species is extremely rare in the Adirondacks and is limited to selected spruce bogs and forests. The Gray Partridge, *Perdix perdix* (AS), found in agricultural areas in the northeastern Adirondacks, was introduced from Europe. It is a smaller bird with a shorter tail, no head crest, a brown face and throat, and a large reddish brown patch on the belly.

Comments: Also known as the Partridge. During mating displays, the male may open his tail like a fan. Also known for the drumming sound of the male, made by beating his wings.

SPRUCE GROUSE
Dendragapus canadensis

Mottled brown and black
Plate 22, No. 3

Length: 15-16 inches
Wingspan: 22-23 inches

Description Male: Upper body mottled with brown, gray and black. Lower body: upper breast black; lower breast and belly white with black bars; sides streaked with brown. Head: top of head and back of neck mottled with brown and black; cheeks and throat black with white edging; a patch of red skin over each eye; bill dark gray to black. Wings heavily variegated with browns and dark gray. Tail broad, nearly black, with dull orange band at tip. Legs completely covered with brown feathers; toes gray.

Description Female: Similar to male but lacks red eye patches, and the solid black plumage of the head and breast is replaced by mottled browns.

Nesting Season: May - June.

Nest: Located on ground in a depression, lined with twigs, leaves and mosses, generally beneath a spruce tree.

Eggs: Four to twelve, pale creamy brown with reddish brown specks, 1.7 inches long by 1.2 inches wide.

Seasonal Status: Permanent resident.

Habitat: Bogs and spruce forests.

Similar Species: The Ruffed Grouse, *Bonasa umbellus* (AS), is a browner bird with a crested head which lacks red eye patches.

Comments: Also known as the Black Grouse. Extremely rare in New York State. It shows little fear of humans.

ROCK DOVE   Gray
Columba livia   Plate 22, No. 4
Length: 12-13 inches
Wingspan: 25 inches

Description Male: Upper body light to dark gray; rump white. Lower body gray; breast with green to purple iridescence. Head gray; neck with green to purple iridescence; bill dark gray with white at base of upper mandible. Wings light to dark gray with two nearly black bands. Tail feathers light to dark gray with nearly black tips forming conspicuous band. Legs pinkish brown. Many color variations commonly occur including white, reddish brown, piebald and combinations of the above.

Description Female: Nearly identical to male.

Nesting Season: May - June (multiple broods may occur).

Nest: Located on man-made structures, loosely constructed of twigs and straw.

Eggs: Two, glossy white, 1.5 inches long by 1.15 inches wide.

Seasonal Status: Permanent resident.

Habitat: Agricultural and populated areas.

Similar Species: No other Adirondack species closely resembles this bird.

Comments: Also known as the Pigeon. Introduced from Europe.

MOURNING DOVE
Zenaida macroura
Length: 11-13 inches
Wingspan: 17-19 inches

Grayish brown
Plate 23, No. 1

Description Male: Upper body grayish brown with olive tints. Lower body tan to light brown with pinkish brown breast. Head grayish brown; back of head and neck bluish tinted; black spot on cheek; sides of neck with greenish iridescence; bill dark brown. Wings grayish brown with bluish gray tips, with a few black spots. Tail long, pointed, dark grayish brown, many feathers with black bars and white tips. Legs reddish brown.

Description Female: Nearly identical to male.

Nesting Season: April - May (multiple broods may occur).

Nest: Located in a bush or tree typically 2-12 feet above ground, loosely constructed of small sticks.

Eggs: Two, white, 1.12 inches long by 0.82 inch wide.

Seasonal Status: Primarily spring, summer and fall with some overwintering.

Habitat: Open fields, agricultural areas, towns and villages.

Similar Species: The now-extinct Passenger Pigeon, *Ectopistes migratorius*, was a larger bird with more grayish coloration on the upper body and grayish brown below. This once extremely common bird became extinct early in the twentieth century, a victim of market hunting.

Comments: Named for its mournful cry. Rapidly increasing its population and range northward since the 1950's. Wings make a whistling sound when it takes off.

NOTES

Section VI

Woodpeckers

Three-toed Woodpecker
Picoides tridactylus

Woodpeckers

Members of the woodpecker family all have strong and sharp bills which they use to drill through wood in search of insect food. They also use their bills to produce loud hammering noises as a part of their reproductive and territorial rituals. Woodpeckers are highly adept at clinging to tree trunks while searching for food.

PILEATED WOODPECKER

Black

Dryocopus pileatus

Plate 23, No. 3

Length: 18-19 inches
Wingspan: 29-30 inches

Description Male: Upper body black. Lower body black with faint white markings along sides. Head black, crested; crest red; often a red patch behind bill; with two white bars, one above eye, one below continuing down side of neck; throat white; bill long, gray. Wings black with few white markings. Tail black. Legs dark gray.

Description Female: Similar to male but lacks red patch behind bill.

Nesting Season: May.

Nest: Located in dead tree cavity drilled by the bird.

Eggs: Three to five, glossy white, 1.3 inches long by 0.96 inch wide.

Seasonal Status: Permanent resident.

Habitat: Deciduous and mixed woodlands.

Similar Species: No other Adirondack species closely resembles this bird.

Comments: The largest Adirondack woodpecker. Despite its large size, it can be an elusive bird. Known for its loud, eerie "jungle-like" call.

COMMON FLICKER
Colaptes auratus

Brown

Plate 23, No. 4; Plate 24, No. 1

Length: 12-13 inches
Wingspan: 19-21.5 inches

Description Male: Upper body brown with slender black bars; rump white. Lower body white with numerous black spots; breast with large black crescent. Head: cap and back of neck gray with a red crescent on back of head; sides and throat pinkish brown; throat edged with black; bill long, sharp, brown. Wing feathers brown with black bars and yellow shafts. Tail feathers dark brown with yellow shafts. Legs dark gray.

Description Female: Similar to male but lacks black throat edging.

Nesting Season: May - June (a second brood may occur).

Nest: Located in cavity in dead tree or limbs, natural or drilled by the Flicker or other bird.

Eggs: Four to eight, white, 1.1 inches long by 0.9 inch wide.

Seasonal Status: Spring, summer and fall.

Habitat: Fields, orchards and woodland edges.

Similar Species: No other Adirondack species closely resembles this bird.

Comments: The only brown-backed woodpecker in the Adirondacks. The only woodpecker to commonly feed on the ground. Has over twenty common names!

BLACK-BACKED WOODPECKER
Picoides arcticus

Black
Plate 24, No. 2

Length: 9.5-10 inches
Wingspan: 14-15 inches

Description Male: Upper body black. Lower body white, sides with many black bars. Head black; crown yellow; forehead white; thin white eye bar; area below cheeks white; throat white with black edges; bill long, sharp, dark gray. Wings black with white spots. Tail black with white edges. Legs gray; feet three-toed.

Description Female: Similar to male but lacks yellow crown.

Nesting Season: May - June.

Nest: Located in cavity of coniferous trees, typically not far from ground.

Eggs: Four to six, white, 1 inch long by 0.7 inch wide.

Seasonal Status: Permanent resident.

Habitat: Bogs in coniferous woodlands.

Similar Species: The Three-toed Woodpecker, *P. tridactylus* (AS), has less yellow on its crown and white bars running down the back. The Yellow-bellied Sapsucker, *Sphyrapicus varius* (Sp, S, F), also has white bars the length of the back, but has a large white wing patch, yellowish belly and red forehead and throat.

Comments: Populations of Three-toed Woodpeckers are rare and localized in the Adirondacks. Eats thousands of harmful wood-boring grubs each year.

RED-HEADED WOODPECKER
Melanerpes erythrocephalus
Length: 9-9.75 inches
Wingspan: 17-18 inches

Black and white
with red head
Plate 24, No. 4

Description Male: Upper body bluish black to black; rump white. Lower body white. Head crimson red; bill long, grayish. Wings black with large white band. Tail black with sparse white margin. Legs dark gray.

Description Female: Nearly identical to male.

Nesting Season: June.

Nest: Located in dead tree cavity drilled by the bird.

Eggs: Four to six, glossy white, 1 inch long by 0.78 inch wide.

Seasonal Status: Spring, summer and fall.

Habitat: Agricultural areas and woodland edges.

Similar Species: No other Adirondack species closely resembles this bird.

Comments: Rarely observed in the Adirondack Park.

DOWNY WOODPECKER
Picoides pubescens

Black and white
Plate 25, No. 1

Length: 6-7 inches
Wingspan: 11.5-12.5 inches

Description Male: Upper body white with black margins. Lower body white. Head black, with bright scarlet patch on back, with white patch above and another below eye; throat white; bill short, sharp, black. Wings black with several white bars. Tail wedge-shaped, mostly black, outer feathers white with black spots. Legs gray.

Description Female: Similar to male but lacks scarlet head patch.

Nesting Season: May - June.

Nest: Located in dead trees or limbs in cavity drilled by the bird, lined with wood chips.

Eggs: Four to six, white, 0.8 inch long by 0.57 inch wide.

Seasonal Status: Permanent resident.

Habitat: Woodlands and orchards.

Similar Species: The Hairy Woodpecker, *P. villosus* (AS), is considerably larger, has a long, sharp bill and lacks black tail spots.

Comments: The smallest American woodpecker.

NOTES

Section VII

Swifts and Swallows

Barn Swallow
Hirundo rustica

Swifts and Swallows

Swallows are small, slender birds with short bills, long pointed wings and usually forked tails. They feed on flying insects and are best known for their exceptionally graceful and fast flying style. The Chimney Swift has even longer wings and a short squared tail.

BARN SWALLOW
Hirundo rustica
Length: 6-7 inches
Wingspan: 12.5-13.5 inches

Steel blue
Plate 25, No. 3

Description Male: Upper body iridescent steel blue. Lower body: breast dark chestnut brown with a blue collar separating it from the pale brown belly. Head iridescent steel blue; forehead and throat dark chestnut brown; bill black. Wings dark steel blue to nearly black. Tail deeply forked, blackish with a band of white spots. Legs black.

Description Female: Nearly identical to male, sometimes with duller plumage.

Nesting Season: May - June (a second brood may occur).

Nest: Typically located in barn rafters and under bridges, constructed of mud and straw.

Eggs: Four to six, white with many brown spots, 0.75 inch long by 0.55 inch wide.

Seasonal Status: Spring, summer and fall.

Habitat: Agricultural areas, creeks, rivers, ponds and lakes.

Similar Species: No other Adirondack swallow has such a deeply forked tail. The Tree Swallow, *Tachycineta bicolor* (Sp, S, F), has a metallic blue upper body, wings and tail, and a white throat and lower body. The Purple Martin, *Progne subis* (Sp, S, F), has glossy purple coloration over its entire body. The Cliff Swallow, *H. pyrrhonota* (Sp, S, F) has a purplish upper body with a yellowish brown rump, a white lower body, a chestnut throat and a squarish tail.

Comments: Capable of killing over 1,000 blackflies per day during nesting season. Vigorous protector of its nest.

BANK SWALLOW   Brown
Riparia riparia   Plate 26, No. 1
Length: 5-5.25 inches
Wingspan: 10.5-11 inches

Description Male: Upper body brown to grayish brown. Lower body white with a brown band across the breast. Head brown to grayish brown; throat white; bill dark brown. Wings and tail slightly darker brown than the upper body. Legs brown.

Description Female: Nearly identical to male.

Nesting Season: May - June (a second brood may occur).

Nest: Located in tunnels in sandy banks, approximately two feet deep, composed of soft grasses and feathers.

Eggs: Four to six, white, 0.68 inch long by 0.5 inch wide.

Seasonal Status: Spring, summer and fall.

Habitat: Creeks, rivers, gravel pits and excavated areas.

Similar Species: The Northern Rough-winged Swallow, *Stelgidopteryx serripennis* (Sp, S, F), lacks the brown breast band and has a dirty white to tan throat and breast. The Chimney Swift, *Chaetura pelagica* (Sp, S, F), has exceptionally long wings, a short squarish tail and dark grayish brown coloration over all body surfaces.

Comments: This bird typically nests in extensive colonies.

Photo Section

Bald Eagle
Haliaeetus leucocephalus

1. Bald Eagle   Page 13
   Haliaeetus leucocephalus

2. Golden Eagle   Page 14
   Aquila chrysaetos

3. Osprey   Page 15
   Pandion haliaetus

4. Rough-legged Hawk   Page 16
   Buteo lagopus

PLATE 2

103

1. Red-tailed Hawk   Page 17
   Buteo jamaicensis

2. Broad-winged Hawk   Page 18
   Buteo platypterus

3. Red-shouldered Hawk   Page 19
   Buteo lineatus

4. Cooper's Hawk   Page 20
   Accipiter cooperii

2. Northern Goshawk   Page 21
   Accipiter gentilis

1. Sharp-shinned Hawk   Page 20
   Accipiter striatus

3. Marsh Hawk   Page 22
   Circus cyaneus

4. Gyrfalcon   Page 23
   Falco rusticolus

PLATE 4 105

1. Peregrine Falcon   Page 24
   Falco peregrinus

2. Merlin   Page 24
   Falco columbarius

3. American Kestrel   Page 25
   Falco sparverius

4. Turkey Vulture   Page 26
   Cathartes aura

1. Black Vulture Page 26
   Coragyps atratus

2. Snowy Owl, male Page 29
   Nyctea scandiaca

3. Snowy Owl, female Page 29
   Nyctea scandiaca

4. Great Horned Owl Page 30
   Bubo virginianus

1. Long-eared Owl   Page 31
   Asio otus

2. Short-eared Owl   Page 32
   Asio flammeus

3. Hawk-Owl   Page 33
   Surnia ulula

4. Great Gray Owl   Page 34
   Strix nebulosa

1. Barred Owl   Page 35
   Strix varia

2. Eastern Screech Owl, gray phase
   Otus asio   Page 36

3. Eastern Screech Owl, red phase
   Otus asio   Page 36

4. Boreal Owl   Page 38
   Aegolius funereus

PLATE 8 109

2. Mute Swan   Page 41
   Cygnus olor

1. Tundra Swan   Page 41
   Olor columbianus

4. Brant   Page 43
   Branta bernicla

3. Canada Goose   Page 42
   Branta canadensis

1. Snow Goose at Sunset   Page 44
   Chen caerulescens

2. Wood Duck   Page 45
   Aix sponsa

3. Black Duck   Page 46
   Anas rubripes

4. Mallard   Page 47
   Anas platyrhynchos

PLATE 10   111

2. Blue-winged Teal   Page 49
   Anas discors

1. Northern Shoveler   Page 48
   Anas clypeata

3. Green-winged Teal   Page 50
   Anas crecca

4. American Wigeon   Page 51
   Anas americana

1. Northern Pintail   Page 52
   Anas acuta

2. Canvasback   Page 53
   Aythya valisineria

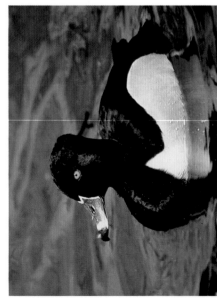

3. Redhead   Page 54
   Aythya americana

4. Ring-necked Duck   Page 55
   Aythya collaris

PLATE 12   113

1. Common Goldeneye   Page 56
   Bucephala clangula

2. Barrow's Goldeneye   Page 56
   Bucephala islandica

3. Bufflehead   Page 57
   Bucephala albeola

4. Common Eider   Page 58
   Somateria mollissima

1. Ruddy Duck   Page 59
   Oxyura jamaicensis

2. Hooded Merganser   Page 60
   Lophodytes cucullatus

3. Common Loon   Page 63
   Gavia immer

4. Double-crested Cormorant Page 64
   Phalacrocorax auritus

PLATE 14   115

1. Ring-billed Gull   Page 65
   Larus delawarensis

2. Herring Gull   Page 65
   Larus argentatus

3. Gull Nesting Colony,   Page 65
   Lake Champlain

4. Gull Chicks in Nest   Page 65

1. Gull Nest and Eggs   Page 65

2. Common Tern   Page 66
   Sterna hirundo

3. Black Tern   Page 66
   Chlidonias niger

4. Glossy Ibis   Page 67
   Plegadis falcinellus

PLATE 16   117

1. Cattle Egret   Page 68
   Bubulcus ibis

2. Great Egret   Page 68
   Casmerodius albus

3. Great Blue Heron   Page 69
   Ardea herodias

4. Little Blue Heron   Page 69
   Egretta caerulea

1. Black-crowned Night-Heron   Page 70
   Nycticorax nycticorax

2. Black-crowned Night-Heron, chicks
   Nycticorax nycticorax   Page 70

3. Yellow-crowned Night-Heron   Page 70
   Nycticorax violaceus

4. Green-backed Heron   Page 71
   Butorides striatus

PLATE 18   119

1. American Bittern   Page 72
   Botaurus lentiginosus

2. Virginia Rail   Page 73
   Rallus limicola

3. Sora   Page 73
   Porzana carolina

4. Common Moorhen   Page 74
   Gallinula chloropus

1. American Coot   Page 75
   Fulica americana

2. Pied-billed Grebe   Page 76
   Podilymbus podiceps

4. Killdeer   Page 77
   Charadrius vociferus

3. Horned Grebe   Page 76
   Podiceps auritus

PLATE 20

121

1. Killdeer, chick and eggs   Page 77
   Charadrius vociferus

2. Spotted Sandpiper   Page 78
   Actitis macularia

4. Sanderling   Page 78
   Calidris alba

3. Upland Sandpiper   Page 78
   Bartramia longicauda

1. American Woodcock   Page 81
   Scolopax minor

2. Common Snipe   Page 81
   Gallinago gallinago

3. Wild Turkey   Page 82
   Meleagris gallapavo

4. Ring-necked Pheasant   Page 83
   Phasianus colchicus

PLATE 22   123

1. Green Pheasant   Page 83
   Phasianus colchicus

2. Ruffed Grouse   Page 84
   Bonasa umbellus

3. Spruce Grouse   Page 85
   Dendragapus canadensis

4. Rock Dove   Page 86
   Columba livia

1. Mourning Dove   Page 87
   Zenaida macroura

2. Passenger Pigeon   Page 87
   Ectopistes migratorius

3. Pileated Woodpecker   Page 91
   Dryocopus pileatus

4. Common Flicker, male   Page 92
   Colaptes auratus

PLATE 24   125

1. Common Flicker, female and young
   Colaptes auratus   Page 92

2. Black-backed Woodpecker   Page 93
   Picoides arcticus

3. Yellow-bellied Sapsucker   Page 93
   Sphyrapicus varius

4. Red-headed Woodpecker   Page 94
   Melanerpes erythrocephalus

1. Downy Woodpecker   Page 95
   Picoides pubescens

2. Hairy Woodpecker   Page 95
   Picoides villosus

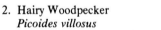

3. Barn Swallow   Page 99
   Hirundo rustica

4. Tree Swallow   Page 99
   Tachycineta bicolor

PLATE 26

127

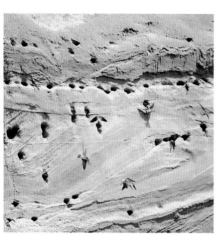

1. Bank Swallow   Page 100
   Riparia riparia

2. Chimney Swift   Page 100
   Chaetura pelagica

3. American Crow   Page 151
   Corvus brachyrhynchos

4. Common Raven   Page 152
   Corvus corax

1. Common Grackle   Page 153
   Quiscalus quiscula

2. Rusty Blackbird   Page 153
   Euphagus carolinus

3. European Starling   Page 154
   Sturnus vulgaris

4. Red-winged Blackbird   Page 155
   Agelaius phoeniceus

PLATE 28   129

1. Brown-headed Cowbird   Page 156
   Molothrus ater

2. Young Brown-headed Cowbird,   Page
   being raised by Yellow Warbler   156

3. Rose-breasted Grosbeak   Page 157
   Pheucticus ludovicianus

4. Rufous-sided Towhee, male   Page 158
   Pipilo erythrophthalmus

1. Rufous-sided Towhee, female at nest
   Pipilo erythrophthalmus   Page 158

2. Eastern Kingbird   Page 159
   Tyrannus tyrannus

3. Bobolink   Page 160
   Dolichonyx oryzivorus

4. Black and White Warbler   Page 161
   Mniotilta varia

PLATE 30   131

1. Northern Oriole   Page 162
   Icterus glabula

2. American Redstart   Page 163
   Setophaga ruticilla

4. Northern Shrike   Page 165
   Lanius excubitor

3. American Robin   Page 164
   Turdus migratorius

1. Gray Jay   Page 166
   Perisoreus canadensis

2. Mockingbird   Page 167
   Mimus polyglottos

3. Catbird   Page 168
   Dumetella carolinensis

4. Tufted Titmouse   Page 169
   Parus bicolor

PLATE 32

133

1. Dark-eyed Junco   Page 170
   Junco hyemalis

2. Black-capped Chickadee Page 171
   Parus atricapillus

3. White-breasted Nuthatch Page 172
   Sitta carolinensis

4. Red-breasted Nuthatch   Page 172
   Sitta canadensis

1. Magnolia Warbler   Page 173
   Dendroica magnolia

2. Yellow-rumped Warbler   Page 173
   Dendroica coronata

3. Northern Parula   Page 173
   Parula americana

4. Black-throated Blue Warbler
   Dendroica caerulescens   Page 174

PLATE 34   135

1. Eastern Bluebird   Page 175
   Sialia sialis

2. Indigo Bunting   Page 176
   Passerina cyanea

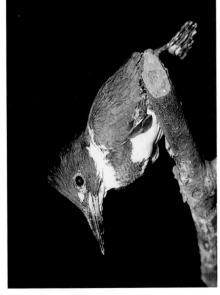

3. Blue Jay   Page 177
   Cyanocitta cristata

4. Belted Kingfisher   Page 178
   Ceryle alcyon

1. Cedar Waxwing   Page 179
   Bombycilla cedrorum

2. Brown Creeper   Page 180
   Certhia americana

3. Lapland Longspur   Page 181
   Calcarius lapponicus

4. House Wren   Page 182
   Troglodytes aedon

PLATE 36   137

1. Long-billed Marsh Wren   Page 182
   Cistothorus palustris

2. Song Sparrow   Page 183
   Melospiza melodia

3. Savannah Sparrow   Page 183
   Passerculus sandwichensis

4. Chipping Sparrow   Page 184
   Spizella passerina

1. Swamp Sparrow   Page 184
   Melospiza georgiana

2. White-throated Sparrow   Page 185
   Zontrichia albicollis

3. White-crowned Sparrow   Page 185
   Zontrichia leucophrys

4. House Sparrow   Page 186
   Passer domesticus

PLATE 38   139

1. Pine Siskin   Page 187
   Carduelis pinus

2. Common Redpoll   Page 188
   Carduelis flammea

3. Snow Bunting   Page 189
   Plectrophenax nivalis

4. Horned Lark   Page 190
   Eremophila alpestris

1. Eastern Meadowlark   Page 191
   Sturnella magna

2. Whip-poor-will   Page 192
   Caprimulgus vociferus

3. Common Nighthawk   Page 192
   Chordeiles minor

4. Black-billed Cuckoo   Page 193
   Coccyzus erythropthalmus

PLATE 40

141

1. Yellow-billed Cuckoo   Page 193
   Coccyzus americanus

2. Brown Thrasher   Page 194
   Toxostoma rufum

4. Wood Thrush   Page 195
   Hylocichla mustelina

3. Hermit Thrush   Page 195
   Catharus guttatus

1. Great Crested Flycatcher　Page 196
   Myiarchus crinitis

2. Willow Flycatcher　Page 197
   Empidonax traillii

3. Eastern Phoebe　Page 197
   Sayornis phoebe

4. Ovenbird　Page 198
   Seiurus aurocapillus

PLATE 42   143

1. Yellow Warbler, Male   Page 199
   Dendroica petechia

2. Yellow Warbler, female at nest   Page 199
   Dendroica petechia

3. Cape May Warbler   Page 199
   Dendroica tigrina

4. Common Yellowthroat   Page 200
   Geothlypis trichas

1. Chestnut-sided Warbler   Page 201
   Dendroica pensylvanica

2. Golden-crowned Kinglet   Page 202
   Regulus satrapa

3. Red-eyed Vireo   Page 203
   Vireo olivaceus

4. Solitary Vireo   Page 203
   Vireo solitarius

PLATE 44

145

1. Ruby-throated Hummingbird, male
   Archilochus colubris   Page 204

2. Ruby-throated Hummingbird, female
   Archilochus colubris   Page 204

3. American Goldfinch   Page 205
   Carduelis tristis

4. Evening Grosbeak   Page 206
   Coccothraustes vespirtinus

1. Pine Grosbeak   Page 207
   Pinicola enucleator

2. White-winged Crossbill   Page 208
   Loxia leucoptera

3. Red Crossbill   Page 209
   Loxia curvirostra

4. House Finch   Page 210
   Carpodacus mexicanus

PLATE 46   147

1. Purple Finch   Page 211
   Carpodacus purpureus

2. Cardinal, male   Page 212
   Cardinalis cardinalis

3. Cardinal, female at nest   Page 212
   Cardinalis cardinalis

4. Scarlet Tanager   Page 213
   Piranga olivacea

NOTES

Section VIII
Perching Birds

Eastern Meadowlark
Sturnella magna

Perching Birds

Perching birds includes all the species that do not belong in any of the previous sections. As their name implies these are the perchers of the bird world, those species typically observed decorating our trees and shrubs. This section includes our best-known and most loved songbirds. Most are small species under ten inches in length, although a few, such as the Crow or Raven, can attain a length of twenty or more inches. Since color is the most important characteristic in identifying these species when using this guide, we have used this feature in arranging this section. The following categories are included: Birds Predominantly Black (including black and white and black and orange), Birds Predominantly any Shade of Gray, Birds Predominantly Blue, Birds Predominantly any Shade of Brown, Birds Predominantly Olive to Green, Birds Predominantly any Shade of Yellow, and Birds Predominantly any Shade of Red.

BIRDS PREDOMINANTLY BLACK

AMERICAN CROW
Corvus brachyrhynchos
Length: 18-20 inches
Wingspan: 35-37 inches

Black
Plate 26, No. 3

Description Male: All parts glossy black with a purplish tinge when viewed in strong sunlight.

Description Female: Nearly identical to male but less glossy.

Nesting Season: April - May.

Nest: Usually located high up in tall trees, lower portion a large, loosely constructed platform of sticks, upper portion composed of small twigs, lined with cedar bark.

Eggs: Four to seven, variable from pale bluish green to much lighter, with brown spots. 1.65 inches long by 1.15 inches wide.

Seasonal Status: Permanent resident, although some are migratory.

Habitat: Woodlands, cultivated fields and grassy areas.

Similar Species: The Common Raven, *C. corax* (AS), is differentiated by its larger size, its High Peaks habitat and its harsher call.

Comments: Groups of crows frequently mob hawks and owls. Frequently mobbed by Red-winged Blackbirds because crows feed on the eggs and young of other birds.

COMMON RAVEN
Corvus corax

Black
Plate 26, No. 4

Length: 24-27 inches
Wingspan: 48-54 inches

Description Male: Upper body glossy black. Lower body a duller black. Head, including throat, black; throat feathers unusually long; bill unusually thick and black. Wings and tail black. Legs black.

Description Female: Nearly identical to male.

Nesting Season: May - June.

Nest: Located in cliffs or very high up in conifers, compactly constructed of large sticks with a lining of soft grasess and animal hairs.

Eggs: Two to seven, bluish green, spotted and streaked with brown, 1.9 inches long by 1.25 inches wide.

Seasonal Status: Permanent resident.

Habitat: The High Peaks Region.

Similar Species: The American Crow, *C. brachyryhnchos* (AS), is differentiated by its smaller size, more widespread distribution and its familiar "caw-caw" call (the Raven has a much harsher "wraw-wraw" call).

Comments: Is considered to be one of the living symbols of the Adirondack Wilderness Area.

COMMON GRACKLE   Black
Quiscalus quiscula   Plate 27, No. 1
Length: 12-13.5 inches
Wingspan: 17-18 inches

Description Male: Upper and lower body iridescent black especially on the back and breast. Head very dark metallic blue; eyes light yellow; bill black. Wings iridescent purplish black. Tail very long and rounded, iridescent purplish black. Legs black.

Description Female: Similar to male, with less iridescence.

Nesting Season: May - June.

Nest: Located in tree hollows, often conifers, 6-60 feet above ground, bulky, constructed of twigs and small vegetation, lined with mud and grass.

Eggs: Three to six, highly variable from greenish or bluish to grayish, spotted and streaked with black to brownish purple, 1.2 inches long by 0.85 inch wide.

Seasonal Status: Permanent resident.

Habitat: Meadows, marshes and areas of human habitation.

Similar Species: The Rusty Blackbird, *Euphagus carolinus* (Sp, S, F), may be differentiated by its smaller size (9.0-9.5 inches long) and by its rusty sheen which is especially pronounced during autumn.

Comments: Also known as the Bronzed Grackle.

EUROPEAN STARLING

Black

Sturnus vulgaris

Plate 27, No. 3

Length: 8-8.5 inches
Wingspan: 12.5-13 inches

Description Male: Upper and lower body black with green and purple tints; individual feathers with slightly paler tips. Head black with greenish purple tints; bill yellow. Wings and tail black with greenish purple tints. Legs brown. In winter, greenish purple tints become much less evident, tips of body feathers become conspicuously grayish white creating a spotted effect, and bill darkens to almost black.

Description Female: Similar to the male but somewhat duller.

Nesting Season: May - June (multiple broods may occur).

Nest: Located in tree hollows, typically 8-50 feet above ground, composed of small sticks and grasses.

Eggs: Four to seven, pale greenish blue to bluish white, 1.13 inches long by 0.83 inch wide.

Seasonal Status: Permanent resident.

Habitat: Woodland edges, grassy areas and areas of human habitation.

Similar Species: The Common Grackle, *Quiscalus quiscula* (AS), is a larger bird with a long tail, unspotted iridescent black plumage and a black bill.

Comments: Originally a native of western Europe. Intentionally introduced into the New York City area in 1890 and is now found in lower 48 states and Alaska. Historical reasons stated for their release range from one man's desire to release as many new species as possible into New York State to a plan that starlings would control local insect pests. It is amusing to note in "Birds of New York," published in 1910, that at that time it was believed there was no danger of the Starling becoming a widespread pest.

RED-WINGED BLACKBIRD
Agelaius phoeniceus
Length: 8-9.5 inches
Wingspan: 15-16 inches

Black
Plate 27, No.4

Description Male: Upper body, lower body, head including bill, tail and legs coal black. Wings coal black with large red shoulder patch edged with yellow.

Description Female: Body brownish with dark brown or blackish streaks.

Nesting Season: May - June.

Nest: Located in low bushes or in heavy vegetation on the ground, composed of weeds and coarse grasses, lined with softer vegetation.

Eggs: Three to five, light blue to greenish blue with dark purple to black spots and patches, 1 inch long by 0.75 inch wide.

Seasonal Status: Spring, summer and fall.

Habitat: Moist meadows, swamps and marshes.

Similar Species: The Rusty Blackbird, *Euphagus carolinus* (Sp, S, F), is black with a rusty sheen and lacks the red shoulder patch.

Comments: Extremely vocal and aggressive when defending its nesting site against intruders, including humans. Will mob crows. Often migrates in large flocks. One of the earliest birds to return in spring.

BROWN-HEADED COWBIRD   Black with brown head
Molothrus ater   Plate 28, No. 1 & 2
Length: 7.5-8 inches
Wingspan: 11.5-13.5 inches

Description Male: Upper and lower body black with iridescent sheen. Head glossy brown; bill dark brown. Wings and tail iridescent black. Legs brownish black.

Description Female: Dull brown, palest on the lower body.

Nesting Season: May - June.

Nest: Employs one of another bird species.

Eggs: Usually one per nest, white with brown and sometimes gray spots, 0.85 inch long by 0.65 inch wide.

Seasonal Status: Spring, summer, fall, occasionally seen in winter.

Habitat: Pasturelands and sparsely forested areas.

Similar Species: The Common Grackle, *Quiscalus quiscula* (AS), is a larger bird with a dark metallic blue head.

Comments: The cowbird does not rear its own young. It deposits one to three eggs in the active nests of Yellow Warblers, Song Sparrows or other species, which then feed and raise the mixed brood. Frequently observed feeding with tail held erect.

———————————————

ROSE-BREASTED GROSBEAK
Pheucticus ludovicianus
Length: 7.75-8.5 inches
Wingspan: 13 inches

Black and white
Plate 28, No. 3

Description Male: Upper body black with a white rump. Lower body white; breast rose red. Head and neck black; bill short, conical and brown. Wings black with two white bars. Tail feathers mostly black, outer feathers black with white edges. Legs brown.

Description Female: Upper body a mixture of light and dark brown. Lower body tan with brown markings. Head brown with white streaks; throat white. Wings brown with two white bars. Tail brown.

Nesting Season: June.

Nest: Located in shrubs and young trees, 5-25 feet above ground, loosely constructed of twigs and fibers, lined with grasses.

Eggs: Three to five, greenish blue to green with brown spots, 0.96 inch long by 0.73 inch wide.

Seasonal Status: Spring, summer and fall.

Habitat: Young woodlands and fields.

Similar Species: The Rufous-sided Towhee, *Pipilo erythrophthalmus* (Sp, S, F), has a solid black back and breast, chestnut brown sides and a black bill.

Comments: Known to eat large numbers of potato beetles and June bugs. Male incubates eggs as much, or more, than female.

RUFOUS-SIDED TOWHEE
Black and white
Pipilo erythrophthalmus   Plate 28, No. 4; Plate 29, No. 1
Length: 8-8.5 inches
Wingspan: 8.5 inches

Description Male: Upper body black. Lower body: upper breast black; lower breast and belly white with chestnut brown sides. Head black; eyes red; bill black. Wings black with white markings. Tail black, outer feathers with white edges. Legs brown.

Description Female: Similar to male but black coloration is replaced with brown.

Nesting Season: May - June.

Nest: Located on ground, constructed of leaves and grasses.

Eggs: Four to five, white with brown specks, 0.95 inch long by 0.72 inch wide.

Seasonal Status: Spring, summer and fall.

Habitat: Woodlands and thickets.

Similar Species: The American Robin, *Turdus migratorius* (Sp, S, F), is larger, has a slate gray to brownish gray upper body and a rusty red lower body.

Comments: The scientific name, *erythrophthalmus* means red eye.

EASTERN KINGBIRD
Tyrannus tyrannus
Length: 8-8.5 inches
Wingspan: 14-15 inches

Black and white
Plate 29, No. 2

Description Male: Upper body dark slate gray. Lower body white with some grayish feathers on the breast. Head black with a concealed orange-red crest on crown; throat white; bill black. Wing feathers black with narrow gray edges. Tail black with white terminal band, outer feathers with white edges. Legs black.

Description Female: Nearly identical to male.

Nesting Season: June - July.

Nest: Located in trees, typically fruit trees, usually 10-25 feet above ground, constructed of weeds and sticks, lined with grasses and animal hair.

Eggs: Three to five, white with brown and gray markings, 0.98 inch long by 0.72 inch wide.

Seasonal Status: Spring, summer and fall.

Habitat: Fields and open areas.

Similar Species: The Loggerhead Shrike, *Lanius ludovicianus* (Sp, S, F), has a lighter gray body, a hooked bill and lacks a white terminal tail band.

Comments: Aggressive defender of its nesting site, attacking larger birds such as crows and hawks that come too close.

BOBOLINK	Black and white
Dolichonyx oryzivorus	Plate 29, No. 3

Length: 6.75-7.25 inches
Wingspan: 12-12.5 inches

Description Male: Upper body: upper back black with buffy yellow streaks; lower back white. Lower body black. Head mostly black; back of head and neck yellowish; bill black. Wing feathers black with dull yellowish edges; wing shoulders white. Tail feathers black with dull yellowish edges. Legs dark brown. In fall and winter colored like the female.

Description Female: Upper body, wings and tail dark brown streaked with yellowish brown. Lower body yellowish brown. Head light brown with two dark brown stripes on crown.

Nesting Season: June.

Nest: Located on the ground in meadows, constructed of grass and leaves.

Eggs: Four to six, grayish with brown spots and streaks, 0.85 inch long by 0.63 inch wide.

Seasonal Status: Spring, summer and fall.

Habitat: Meadows.

Similar Species: No other Adirondack species closely resembles this bird.

Comments: Consumes large quantities of insects.

BLACK AND WHITE WARBLER　　　Black and white
Mniotilta varia　　　　　　　　　　Plate 29, No. 4

Length: 5-5.25 inches
Wingspan: 8.5 inches

Description Male: Upper body covered with black and white stripes. Lower body white with black stripes on sides of belly. Head with black and white stripes; throat and bill black. Wings and tail black with white markings. Legs dark gray.

Description Female: Similar to male, but with white throat.

Nesting Season: June.

Nest: Located on the ground, constructed of leaves and grass, lined with hairs.

Eggs: Three to five, white with brown spots at larger end, 0.65 inch long by 0.55 inch wide.

Seasonal Status: Spring, summer and fall.

Habitat: Woodlands.

Similar Species: The Blackburnian Warbler, *Dendroica fusca* (Sp, S, F), is nearly identical but has black and orange facial coloration.

Comments: Also known as the Black and White Creeper because it clings to the trunks of trees in the same manner as the Nuthatch and Brown Creeper.

NORTHERN ORIOLE
Icterus galbula
Length: 7-8 inches
Wingspan: 11.0-12.25 inches

Black and orange
Plate 30, No. 1

Description Male: Upper body: upper back black; lower back orange. Lower body: breast black; belly brilliant orange. Head black; bill black. Wings black with white markings. Tail black, outer feathers orange on lower half. Legs slate gray.

Description Female: Upper body and head olive brown; lower body dull yellow. Wings brown with white markings. Tail olive brown.

Nesting Season: May - June.

Nest: Suspended from tree branches, 8-25 feet above ground, basket-like, tightly woven from plant fibers, animal hairs and often string.

Eggs: Three to five, bluish white with irregular brown lines, 0.92 inch long by 0.62 inch wide.

Seasonal Status: Spring, summer and fall.

Habitat: Open areas with some large trees, often near areas of human habitation.

Similar Species: The American Redstart, *Setophaga ruticilla* (Sp, S, F), is smaller, has a white belly and lacks white wing markings.

Comments: No other bird found in the Adirondacks shares the brilliant orange coloration of the Northern Oriole. Formerly known as the Baltimore Oriole.

AMERICAN REDSTART Black and orange
Setophaga ruticilla Plate 30, No. 2
Length: 5-5.5 inches
Wingspan: 7.5-8 inches

Description Male: Upper body glossy black. Lower body: breast glossy black; belly white with salmon orange sides. Head glossy black; bill black. Wings black with an orange band. Tail black, upper half of outer feathers orange. Legs black.

Description Female: Similar to the male, but the black is replaced by olive gray and the orange is replaced by light yellow.

Nesting Season: June - July.

Nest: Located in trees, 10-30 feet above ground, constructed of grasses and mosses.

Eggs: Three to five, white with numerous brownish spots, 0.66 inch long by 0.51 inch wide.

Seasonal Status: Spring, summer and fall.

Habitat: Damp woodlands.

Similar Species: The Northern Oriole, *Icterus galbula* (Sp, S, F), is larger, has an orange belly and white wing markings.

Comments: One of the most active warblers, constantly fluttering about the underbrush in pursuit of flying insects.

BIRDS PREDOMINANTLY
ANY SHADE OF GRAY

AMERICAN ROBIN Slate gray and rusty red
Turdus migratorius Plate 30, No. 3
Length: 10 inches
Wingspan: 16 inches

Description Male: Upper body slate gray to brownish gray. Lower body rusty red except for white area near tail. Head top and sides nearly black; eyes ringed with white; throat white with dark brown streaks; bill yellow. Wings dark brown. Tail brownish black with white tips on corners. Legs brown.

Description Female: Similar to male but paler.

Nesting Season: May (a second brood may occur).

Nest: Located in trees and shrubs, typically 5-35 feet above ground, composed of leaves and grasses cemented with an inner wall of mud.

Eggs: Three to five, pale greenish blue, 1.15 inches long by 0.8 inch wide.

Seasonal Status: Spring, summer and fall.

Habitat: Young woodlands and open grassy areas.

Similar Species: No other Adirondack species closely resembles this bird.

Comments: An anxiously anticipated sign of spring.

NORTHERN SHRIKE
Gray

Lanius excubitor
Plate 30, No. 4

Length: 9-10.3 inches
Wingspan: 14-15 inches

Description Male: Upper body bluish gray to ash gray. Lower body light gray with darker indistinct wavy lines. Head bluish gray to ash gray; throat light gray, with a distinct black bar around and behind each eye; bill large, hooked downward and black. Wings black with a white spot. Tail black with white outer feathers. Legs black.

Description Female: Nearly identical to male.

Nesting Season: This bird is not known to nest in the Adirondacks.

Nest: Not applicable.

Eggs: Not applicable.

Seasonal Status: Winter visitant.

Habitat: Edges of woodlands and hedgerows.

Similar Species: The Loggerhead Shrike, *L. ludovicianus* (Sp, S, F), may be differentiated by its smaller size (9.0 inches) and its lighter gray coloration. The black eye marking is continuous and meets over the bill.

Comments: A carnivorous species best known for its habit of impaling insects, snakes, small birds and mammals on the sharp thorns of hawthorn trees and shrubs.

GRAY JAY   Gray
Perisoreus canadensis   Plate 31, No. 1
Length: 11-12 inches
Wingspan: 15-17 inches

Description Male: Upper body gray. Lower body light gray. Head: crown, cheeks and throat white; back nearly black; bill dark gray. Wings dark gray. Tail feathers dark gray with a few white tips. Legs dark gray.

Description Female: Nearly identical to male.

Nesting Season: March - April.

Nest: Located in the lower branches of conifer trees, composed of twigs and bark with a lining of mosses and feathers.

Eggs: Four to six, grayish white with faint brown spots, 1.12 inches long by 0.8 inch wide.

Seasonal Status: Permanent resident.

Habitat: Coniferous forests.

Similar Species: The Northern Shrike, *Lanius excubitor* (W), has black wings and tail and a black eye mask.

Comments: Sometimes becomes quite bold when visiting campsites in search of a meal. Also known as the Camp Robber.

MOCKINGBIRD
Mimus polyglottos

Gray
Plate 31, No. 2

Length: 9-10.5 inches
Wingspan: 12-13 inches

Description Male: Upper body ashy gray. Lower body grayish white. Head ashy gray; throat white; bill black. Wings brownish gray with white shoulder patch that is especially conspicuous during flight. Tail long, dark brownish gray with outer three feathers white on each side. Legs black.

Description Female: Similar to male, slightly paler.

Nesting Season: May.

Nest: Located in bushes and lower tree branches, loosely constructed of twigs, strips of bark, weeds and sometimes cloth.

Eggs: Four to six, bluish or greenish with reddish brown spots, 0.95 inch long by 0.7 inch wide.

Seasonal Status: Spring, summer and fall.

Habitat: Fields and woodlands.

Similar Species: The Catbird, *Dumetella carolinensis* (Sp, S, F), may be differentiated by its darker gray coloration and the absence of white markings.

Comments: Named for its ability to mimic the calls of other birds.

CATBIRD
Dumetella carolinensis

Slate gray
Plate 31, No. 3

Length: 8-9 inches
Wingspan: 11-12 inches

Description Male: Upper body slate gray. Lower body lighter gray with a chestnut patch near the tail. Head slate gray with dull black crown; bill black. Wings slate gray. Tail long and slate gray. Legs black.

Description Female: Nearly identical to male.

Nesting Season: May (a second brood may occur).

Nest: Located in low bushes, raggedly constructed of sticks and bark, lined with softer vegetation.

Eggs: Three to six, glossy greenish blue, 0.95 inch long by 0.7 inch wide.

Seasonal Status: Spring, summer and fall.

Habitat: Woodlands.

Similar Species: The Mockingbird, *Mimus polyglottos* (Sp, S, F), may be differentiated by its lighter gray color and conspicuous white markings.

Comments: Named for its piercing cat-like cry. Also has the ability to mimic the calls of other birds.

TUFTED TITMOUSE
Parus bicolor

Light gray
Plate 31, No. 4

Length: 6-6.5 inches
Wingspan: 10-10.75 inches

Description Male: Upper body light gray. Lower body grayish white; sides of belly pale reddish brown. Head crested, light gray; cheeks and throat grayish white, forehead black, bill dark gray. Wings and tail slightly darker gray than back. Legs gray.

Description Female: Nearly identical to male.

Nesting Season: This species is not known to nest in the Adirondacks.

Nest: Not applicable.

Eggs: Not applicable.

Seasonal Status: Can be observed during all seasons.

Habitat: Woodlands.

Similar Species: The Dark-eyed Junco, *Junco hyemalis* (AS), is darker gray and lacks a head crest.

Comments: Known to eat harmful insects such as tent caterpillar eggs, scale insects and sawflies.

DARK-EYED JUNCO
Junco hyemalis

Slate gray
Plate 32, No. 1

Length: 6-6.25 inches
Wingspan: 9.75 inches

Description Male: Upper body slate gray. Lower body: breast slate gray; belly white. Head dark slate gray; bill flesh-colored. Wings dark slate gray. Tail dark slate gray with white outer feathers that flash conspicuously during flight. Legs light brown.

Description Female: Similar to the male, with a brownish tinge over the gray colorations.

Nesting Season: June (a second brood may occur).

Nest: Located on the ground, constructed of grasses, mosses and animal hairs.

Eggs: Four to six, off-white with brown spots, 0.75 inch long by 0.55 inch wide.

Seasonal Status: Permanent resident.

Habitat: Cultivated fields, roadsides and woodlands.

Similar Species: The Black-capped Chickadee, *Parus atricapillus* (AS), has a black cap and throat. The Tufted Titmous, *P. bicolor* (AS), is paler gray and has a conspicuous head crest.

Comments: Also known as the Slate-colored Junco.

BLACK-CAPPED CHICKADEE
Parus atricapillus
Length: 5-5.25
Wingspan: 8.05 inches

Light gray with
black crest
Plate 32, No. 2

Description Male: Upper body light gray, sometimes with brownish tints. Lower body dull white except white on central breast. Head: top, back of neck, throat and bill black; sides white. Wing and tail feathers lead gray with white edges. Legs dark gray.

Description Female: Nearly identical to male.

Nesting Season: May - June.

Nest: Located in tree cavity or abandoned woodpecker hole, constructed entirely of soft materials such as mosses, feathers, furs and plant fibers.

Eggs: Five to eight, white with sparse light brown specks, 0.57 inch long by 0.47 inch wide.

Seasonal Status: Permanent resident.

Habitat: Woodlands and orchards.

Similar Species: The Boreal Chickadee, *P. hudsonicus* (AS), has a brownish to grayish brown upper body and cap and brownish to reddish brown sides on the lower body. The Dark-eyed Junco, *Junco hyemalis* (AS), has a completely gray head and throat.

Comments: Easily attracted to feeders containing suet or sunflower seeds.

WHITE-BREASTED NUTHATCH
Sitta carolinensis

Bluish gray
Plate 32, No. 3

Length: 5.75-6.1 inches
Wingspan: 10.5-11 inches

Description Male: Upper body gray to bluish gray. Lower body white becoming reddish brown near tail. Head and throat white; crown from bill to back of neck black; bill long, slender and black. Wing feathers slate gray with black to brownish edges. Tail short, gray with black and white markings. Legs dark gray.

Description Female: Similar to male, but black on crown replaced by dark bluish gray.

Nesting Season: May.

Nest: Located in tree cavity or abandoned woodpecker hole, constructed of soft feathers, leaves and animal hairs.

Eggs: Five to ten, white with many reddish brown specks, 0.77 inch long by 0.56 inch wide.

Seasonal Status: Permanent resident.

Habitat: Deciduous and mixed woodlands.

Similar Species: The Red-breasted Nuthatch, *S. canadensis* (AS), is slightly smaller, has a prominent black eye bar and a light reddish brown lower body.

Comments: Nuthatches are commonly observed clinging upside down on trees. Finds insects that woodpeckers miss by traveling down trees rather than up them.

MAGNOLIA WARBLER
Dendroica magnolia
Length: 4.8-5.1 inches
Wingspan: 7-7.5 inches

Gray and yellow
Plate 33, No. 1

Description Male: Upper body dark gray to black; rump bright yellow. Lower body bright yellow with prominent black streaks. Head: crown and back of neck ashy gray, with a black mask enclosing forehead, most of the eye region and cheeks; a thin grayish white line separates the gray from the black above and behind the eye; throat bright yellow; bill black. Wings nearly black with a white shoulder patch. Tail nearly black with several white markings. Legs dark gray.

Description Female: Similar to male, but black areas replaced by dark brown.

Nesting Season: June.

Nest: Located in coniferous trees, typically 5-15 feet above ground, constructed of grasses, pine needles and weeds.

Eggs: Four to five, white with brown markings at larger end, 0.65 inch long by 0.48 inch wide.

Seasonal Status: Spring, summer and fall.

Habitat: Coniferous woodlands.

Similar Species: The Yellow-rumped Warbler, *D. coronata* (Sp, S, F), has a white belly and throat and a yellow crown and rump. The Northern Parula *Parula americana* (Sp, S, F), has a bluish gray upper body, head, wings and tail, lacks black face mask and breast streaks and has a white lower belly. The Canada Warbler, *Wilsonia canadensis* (Sp, S, F), has a slate gray upper body and head, yellow throat and lower body and a few short black streaks on the upper breast.

Comments: Mid-level species, tending to stay between 5-20 feet in trees when feeding.

BLACK-THROATED BLUE WARBLER
Dendroica caerulescens

Bluish gray
Plate 33, No. 4

Length: 5-5.25 inches
Wingspan: 8.5 inches

Description Male: Upper body bluish gray. Lower body white with black sides. Head: crown and back bluish gray, remaining portions including throat and bill black. Wings various shades of bluish gray, with white patch. Tail dark bluish gray with scattered white markings. Legs brownish.

Description Female: Upper body grayish brown with olive hues. Lower body pale yellow. Head olive brown; throat light yellow, with a thin white line from the bill to above and behind the eye.

Nesting Season: June.

Nest: Located in hemlock or yew, typically close to the ground, constructed of grasses and pine needles, lined with hairs and soft vegetation.

Eggs: Three to four, white with brownish markings at large end, 0.72 inch long by 0.5 inch wide.

Seasonal Status: Spring, summer and fall.

Habitat: Mixed woodlands.

Similar Species: No other species of warbler found in the Adirondacks has this combination of colors.

Comments: Female feigns injury to draw predators away from the nest.

BIRDS PREDOMINANTLY BLUE

EASTERN BLUEBIRD
Sialia sialis
Length: 7 inches
Wingspan: 12-13 inches

Blue
Plate 34, No. 1

Description Male: Upper body bright blue. Lower body chestnut to brick red becoming white on the belly. Head bright blue; throat chestnut; bill black. Wings and tail bright blue. Legs black.

Description Female: Similar to the male, duller blue on upper body, paler on lower body.

Nesting Season: May (a second brood may occur).

Nest: Located in tree cavities or bird houses, composed of soft grasses.

Eggs: Three to six, usually pale blue, occasionally white, 0.84 inch long by 0.62 inch wide.

Seasonal Status: Spring, summer and fall.

Habitat: Young woodlands and open fields.

Similar Species: The Indigo Bunting, *Passerina cyanea* (Sp, S, F), is smaller and has distinctly iridescent blue plumage.

Comments: State bird of New York. Following a sharp decline in population due to loss of nesting habitats, an intensive program of providing specially constructed nesting boxes has dramatically increased their numbers.

INDIGO BUNTING
Passerina cyanea
Length: 5.5 inches
Wingspan: 8.5 inches

Blue
Plate 34, No. 2

Description Male: Upper and lower body iridescent indigo blue. Head bright iridescent indigo blue; upper mandible bluish brown; lower mandible pale grayish blue. Wing and tail feathers brown with bluish edges. Legs brown. In winter, wings and tail take on a browner cast.

Description Female: Upper body and head light brown. Lower body brownish gray with faint darker brown streaks. Wings and tail darker brown.

Nesting Season: June (a second brood may occur).

Nest: Located in low bushes, often very close to the ground, constructed of leaves and grasses.

Eggs: Three to four, usually white, occasionally blue tinted with brown spots, 0.79 inch long by 0.58 inch wide.

Seasonal Status: Spring, summer and fall.

Habitat: Overgrown pastures and edges of woodlands.

Similar Species: The Eastern Bluebird, *Sialia sialis* (Sp, S, F), may be differentiated by its larger size and chestnut colored breast.

Comments: Although some books state the male does not feed the young, our experience at numerous nesting sites (8), refutes this claim.

BLUE JAY
Blue

Cyanocitta cristata
Plate 34, No. 3

Length: 11-12 inches
Wingspan: 15.5-17 inches

Description Male: Upper body grayish blue. Lower body grayish white. Head with pointed grayish blue crest; throat and sides grayish white; neck collar black; bill black. Wings bright blue, many feathers with black bars and white tips. Tail bright blue, many feathers with black bars and white tips. Legs black.

Description Female: Nearly identical to male, coloration sometimes slightly subdued.

Nesting Season: April - May.

Nest: Usually located in conifers typically 5-45 feet above ground, loosely constructed of twigs and weeds, sometimes string or cloth.

Eggs: Three to six, greenish to yellowish green with reddish brown to lilac spots, 1.1 inches long by 0.8 inch wide.

Seasonal Status: Permanent resident.

Habitat: Woodlands.

Similar Species: The Belted Kingfisher, *Ceryle alcyon* (Sp, S, F), has a shorter tail and blue breast band.

Comments: Frequent visitor to bird feeders but aggressive, often driving other birds away. Can be extremely vocal, especially when disturbed, alerting other animals in the area to potential danger. Frequently feeds on eggs and young of other birds.

BELTED KINGFISHER   Blue
Ceryle alcyon   Plate 34, No. 4
Length: 13 inches
Wingspan: 22 inches

Description Male: Upper body grayish blue. Lower body white, with a broad, blue breast band. Head disproportionately large, with a prominent crest, bluish gray with a white spot in front of each eye; neck collar white; bill long, massive and dark bluish gray. Wing feathers grayish blue with white tips. Tail feathers grayish blue with white spots. Legs grayish.

Description Female: Similar to the male, with a bright chestnut band across the belly.

Nesting Season: May - June.

Nest: Located in the ground in 3-6 feet deep burrows excavated by the mated pair, occasionally lined with grasses.

Eggs: Five to eight, white, 1.35 inches long by 1.05 inches wide.

Seasonal Status: Spring, summer and fall.

Habitat: Along ponds, lakes, streams and rivers.

Similar Species: The Blue Jay, *Cyanocitta cristata* (AS), has a distinctly longer tail and a black neck collar.

Comments: Highly skilled at diving and fishing for minnows. Will also consume frogs and crayfish.

BIRDS PREDOMINANTLY
ANY SHADE OF BROWN

CEDAR WAXWING
Bombycilla cedrorum

Light brown
Plate 35, No. 1

Length: 6.75-7.25 inches
Wingspan: 11-11.5 inches

Description Male: Upper body brown shading to gray on rump. Lower body cinnamon brown shading to yellowish on belly. Head crested, cinnamon brown; eyes enclosed in black bar extending from bill to back of crest; bill black. Wings grayish brown with small red area near center. Tail feathers grayish with yellow tips, forming a solid yellow band. Legs dark gray.

Description Female: Similar to male, with slightly duller plumage.

Nesting Season: June - August.

Nest: Located in trees, 6-25 feet above ground, constructed of twigs and soft grasses.

Eggs: Three to five, light bluish gray with black spots, 0.85 inch long by 0.6 inch wide.

Seasonal Status: Spring, summer and fall; occasionally seen in winter.

Habitat: Young woodlands.

Similar Species: The Bohemian Waxwing, *B. garrulus* (W), is a rare winter visitant and may be differentiated by a long yellow wing bar and a brownish belly which shades to rusty brown near the tail.

Comments: The name Cedar Waxwing derives from the habit of feeding on cedar seeds and from the small wax-like red area on the wings. Begins nesting later than most other birds.

BROWN CREEPER
Certhia americana
Length: 5-5.6 inches
Wingspan: 7.5-8 inches

Brown
Plate 35, No. 2

Description Male: Upper body dark brown, heavily marked with light brown and grayish brown, becoming reddish brown towards tail. Lower body white. Head dark brown, heavily marked with light brown, with a white bar above eye; throat white; bill long, slender, curved downward and brown. Wings dark brown with light brown bands, many feathers white-tipped. Tail long, grayish brown to pale brown. Legs brown.

Description Female: Nearly identical to male.

Nesting Season: May (a second brood may occur).

Nest: Located under large strips of loose bark, constructed of soft materials such as mosses, feathers, and spider and insect cocoons.

Eggs: Five to eight, off-white with some reddish brown spotting at larger end, 0.59 inch long by 0.47 inch wide.

Seasonal Status: Permanent resident, although some migrate south during winter.

Habitat: Moist mixed woodlands.

Similar Species: No other Adirondack brown bird of similar size feeds while clinging and creeping along tree trunks.

Comments: Formerly known as *C. familiaris*. It feeds on insects while clinging and creeping along tree trunks. Typically feeds in a spiral pattern.

LAPLAND LONGSPUR
Calcarius lapponicus
Length: 6.25-6.5 inches
Wingspan: 10.5-11.25 inches

Brown
Plate 35, No. 3

Description Male: Upper body brown with brownish black streaks. Lower body grayish white with few faint black streaks. Head brown with brownish black streaks, with small chestnut brown patch on back of neck; throat grayish white; bill yellowish brown with darker tip. Wing feathers a mixture of light and dark brown. Tail dark brown, outer feathers with white edges. Legs grayish black; feet with conspicuously long spur.

Description Female: Nearly identical to male.

Nesting Seasson: This bird is not known to nest in the Adirondacks.

Nest: Not applicable.

Eggs: Not applicable.

Seasonal Status: Winter resident.

Habitat: Fields and other open areas.

Similar Species: Most other sparrow-like birds differ from the Lapland Longspur by their shorter foot spurs. The Snow Bunting, *Plectrophenax nivalis* (W), which also has a conspicuously long foot spur, may be differentiated by its lighter colored body and absence of black breast markings.

Comments: Sometimes observed feeding beside Snow Buntings and Horned Larks.

HOUSE WREN
Troglodytes aedon
Length: 5 inches
Wingspan: 6.75 inches

Brown
Plate 35, No. 4

Description Male: Upper body brown with faint blackish bars. Lower body grayish to tan with brown side bars. Head brown; throat grayish; bill long and thin; upper mandible dark brown; lower mandible tan. Wings brown with faint blackish bands. Tail rounded, often held erect, brown with faint blackish bands. Legs brown.

Description Female: Nearly identical to male.

Nesting Season: May (multiple broods may occur).

Nest: Located in tree cavity, constructed of twigs and grasses, lined with feathers.

Eggs: Six to eight, white, densely covered with reddish brown markings, 0.6 inch long by 0.48 inch wide.

Seasonal Status: Spring, summer and fall.

Habitat: Orchards, farmlands, towns and villages.

Similar Species: The Winter Wren, *T. troglodytes* (Sp, S, F), is a forest resident which may be differentiated by its extremely short, stubby tail. The Long-billed Marsh Wren, *Cistothorus palustris* (Sp, S, F), is a resident of cattail marshes and has a white belly and conspicuous white bar over the eye . The rare Short-billed Marsh Wren, *C. platensis* (Sp, S, F), is the only Adirondack wren with a streaked crown.

Comments: A key identification feature of all wrens is the typically erect tail. Frequently use Bluebird nesting boxes. Often claim many boxes by laying a single egg in each, which they later abandon. Raise their young in only one box.

SPARROWS WITH CONSPICUOUSLY STREAKED BREASTS

SONG SPARROW
Melospiza melodia
Length: 6-6.4 inches
Wingspan: 8-8.75

Brown
Plate 36, No. 2

Description Male: Upper body brown to reddish brown, streaked with darker brown. Lower body grayish white; breast and sides of belly heavily streaked with dark brown to blackish, conspicuous dark brown to blackish spot in center of breast. Head brown, streaked with darker brown and gray; throat grayish white with dark brown streaks on sides; bill brown. Wings brown with blackish markings. Tail and legs brown.

Description Female: Nearly identical to male.

Nesting Season: May (multiple broods may occur).

Nest: Located on the ground or in low shrubs, variably constructed of grasses, weeds, leaves and bark.

Eggs: Four to five, white with irregular brownish markings, 0.76-0.85 inch long by 0.55-0.6 inch wide.

Seasonal Status: Permanent resident.

Habitat: Meadows and swampy areas.

Similar Species: The Savannah Sparrow, *Passerculus sandwichensis* (Sp, S, F), lacks the conspicuous breast spot and has a yellowish eye bar. The Vesper Sparrow, *Pooecetes gramineus* (Sp, S, F), lacks the conspicuous breast spot and has a white eye ring and white outer tail feathers. The Fox Sparrow, *Passerella iliaca* (Sp, F), lacks the conspicuous breast spot, and has reddish tints, especially noticeable on the tail.

Comments: Known for its beautiful singing.

SPARROWS LACKING A
CONSPICUOUSLY STREAKED BREAST

CHIPPING SPARROW
Spizella passerina

Brown
Plate 36, No. 4

Length: 5-5.4 inches
Wingspan: 8.75 inches

Description Male: Upper body light brown with dark brown to blackish streaks. Lower body light gray. Head: crown chestnut brown; black eye bar; area between eye bar and crown white; lower head and throat grayish white; bill dark gray. Wings brown with blackish markings. Tail dark brown. Legs pale brown. In winter, the head becomes streaked dull brown.

Description Female: Nearly identical to male.

Nesting Season: May (a second brood may occur).

Nest: Located in a bush or tree, 1-25 feet above ground, constructed of grasses, lined with horse hairs.

Eggs: Three to five, bluish with brown markings, 0.7 inch long by 0.51 inch wide.

Seasonal Status: Spring, summer and fall.

Habitat: Fields and cultivated areas.

Similar Species: The Field Sparrow, *S. pusilla* (Sp, S, F), lacks the black and white facial markings and has a pinkish bill. The Tree Sparrow, *S. arborea* (F, W, Sp), also lacks the black and white facial markings and has a conspicuous black spot on its breast. The Swamp Sparrow, *Melospiza georgiana* (Sp, S, F), is a darker brown species with a distinct white throat patch. The Grasshopper Sparrow, *Ammodramus savannarum* (Sp, S, F), has a yellowish breast and a streaked, dull brown crest.

Comments: A favorite of farmers because it feeds heavily on destructive insect larvae, especially caterpillars.

WHITE-THROATED SPARROW
Zonotrichia albicollis

Brown
Plate 37, No. 2

Length: 6.5-6.75 inches
Wingspan: 9.5-10 inches

Description Male: Upper body brown to reddish brown with dark brown streaks. Lower body: breast light gray, becoming white on belly. Head: cheeks gray; crown white-edged with black; conspicuous yellow spot between eye and bill; black eye bar; area between eye bar and crown white; throat white; bill gray. Wings reddish brown with dark brown edges, with two white shoulder bars. Tail brown. Legs pinkish brown.

Description Female: Nearly identical to male.

Nesting Season: May - June (a second brood may occur).

Nest: Located on the ground or in low shrubs, composed of grasses and weeds.

Eggs: Four to five, whitish with irregular pinkish brown markings, 0.79-0.89 inch long by 0.61-0.64 inch wide.

Seasonal Status: Permanent resident.

Habitat: Coniferous woodlands to roadside thickets.

Similar Species: The White-crowned Sparrow, *Z. leucophrys* (Sp, F), is a migratory visitant which lacks the yellow head spot and has a gray throat.

Comments: Thought to be the Adirondacks most handsome sparrow.

HOUSE SPARROW
Passer domesticus

Grayish brown
Plate 37, No. 4

Length: 6-6.3 inches
Wingspan: 9.5-10 inches

Description Male: Upper body brown to grayish brown with black streaks. Lower body: upper breast black; lower breast and belly grayish. Head: cap and cheeks gray, with band of chestnut brown from eye to back of head, a white area between throat and cheeks; throat black; bill dark gray. Wings brown with white shoulder bar edged in chestnut. Tail and legs brown.

Description Female: Similar to male but gray and black areas replaced by dull brown.

Nesting Season: April (multiple broods may occur).

Nest: Located in roof overhangs or in trees, composed of grasses and weeds.

Eggs: Four to six, white to greenish white with brown to gray markings, 0.8 inch long by 0.6 inch wide.

Seasonal Status: Permanent resident.

Habitat: Towns, villages and farms.

Similar Species: No other Adirondack sparrow has a gray cap and black throat.

Comments: Formerly known as the English Sparrow. Released in New York City in 1851 and has expanded its range to the entire country.

PINE SISKIN
Carduelis pinus
Length: 4.75-5 inches
Wingspan: 8.5-8.65 inches

Grayish brown
Plate 38, No. 1

Description Male: Upper body grayish brown with dark brown streaks, becoming yellowish on the rump. Lower body light grayish brown streaked with brown. Head light brown with darker brown streaks; bill brown. Wings dark brown with two shoulder bars, one tan, one sulphur yellow. Tail forked, feathers dark brown, outer feathers with yellow bases. Legs brown.

Description Female: Nearly identical to male.

Nesting Season: April - May.

Nest: Located very high in conifer trees, composed of grasses and pine needles.

Eggs: Four, greenish blue with brown speckles, 0.68 inch long by 0.48 inch wide.

Seasonal Status: Primarily a winter resident; however, small populations may be observed throughout spring, summer and fall.

Habitat: Coniferous woodlands.

Similar Species: The American Goldfinch, *C. tristis* (AS), has a solid yellow upper and lower body and a yellow, black-capped head.

Comments: Identifying yellow colorations are most easily observed during flight. Although limited nesting occurs in the Adirondacks, the primary nesting grounds are further north.

COMMON REDPOLL Grayish brown
Carduelis flammea Plate 38, No. 2
Length: 5.25-5.5 inches
Wingspan: 8.25-8.75 inches

Description Male: Upper body grayish brown, heavily streaked with darker brown; pinkish tinged on rump. Lower body off-white streaked with brown; breast pink. Head grayish brown with dark brown markings; crown red; throat black; bill light brown. Wings brown with two white shoulder bars. Tail brown. Legs brown. Pinkish tints more subdued in winter.

Description Female: Similar to male but lacking pink tints on rump and breast.

Nesting Season: This bird is not known to nest in the Adirondacks.

Nest: Not applicable.

Eggs: Not applicable.

Seasonal Status: Winter visitant.

Habitat: Meadows and cultivated fields.

Similar Species: The Purple Finch, *Carpodacus purpureus* (AS), and the House Finch, *C. mexicanus* (AS), may appear similar but lack the black throat patch of the Common Redpoll.

Comments: Breeds in summer in the far northern regions of Canada.

SNOW BUNTING
Plectrophenax nivalis
Length: 6.75-7.25 inches
Wingspan: 6-6.5 inches

Grayish brown and white
Plate 38, No. 3

Description Male: Upper body grayish brown with black markings. Lower body white with an indistinct brown collar on the breast. Head white; crown, cheeks and back of head light brown; bill light brown. Wings white with black tip. Tail black and white. Legs black.

Description Female: Similar to male but brown coloration is less intense.

Nesting Season: This bird is not known to nest in the Adirondacks.

Nest: Not applicable.

Eggs: Not applicable.

Seasonal Status: Winter resident.

Habitat: Fields and other open areas.

Similar Species: The Hoary Redpoll, *Carduelis hornemanni* (W), is a rare winter visitant which has brown streaks on the upper body and a red crown.

Comments: This species nests in the Arctic Circle during the summer months.

HORNED LARK

Eremophila alpestris

Brown
Plate 38, No. 4

Length: 7.5-8 inches
Wingspan: 11-12 inches

Description Male: Upper body a mixture of light and dark brown. Lower body tan; upper breast covered with a large black crescent; lower breast with scattered dark brown markings. Head light brown with two black horn-like tufts of feathers on the crown, with a black streak from the bill to the eye and down the cheek; area above and behind the eye white to pale yellow; throat yellow; bill dark brown. Wing feathers brown with paler edges. Tail feathers mostly brown, outer tail feathers nearly black with white edges. Legs dark brown.

Description Female: Similar to the male, paler and with less black.

Nesting Season: April - May (a second brood may occur).

Nest: Located on ground, loosely constructed of grasses.

Eggs: Four, grayish white with many light brown spots, 0.85 inch long by 0.63 inch wide.

Seasonal Status: Permanent resident.

Habitat: Meadows and farmers' fields.

Similar Species: The Eastern Meadowlark, *Sturnella magna* (Sp, S, F), also displays a prominent black breast crescent, but lacks head tufts.

Comments: Because it nests on the ground so early in the year, the first brood may be destroyed by late season snowfall.

EASTERN MEADOWLARK   Brown and yellow
Sturnella magna   Plate 39, No. 1
Length: 10-11 inches
Wingspan: 14-16.5 inches

Description Male: Upper body brown with black markings. Lower body bright yellow with dark brown markings and streaks near the wings; breast covered with a large black crescent. Head light brown with two dark brown streaks on each side; area in front of eye and throat bright yellow; bill brown. Wings brown with black markings. Tail short, mostly brown with black markings, outer feathers white. Legs brown. Plumage duller in winter.

Description Female: Similar to the male, often paler.

Nesting Season: May - June.

Nest: Located on the ground, composed of woven grasses, arched over.

Eggs: Four to six, white speckled with reddish brown, 1.1 inches long by 0.8 inch wide.

Seasonal Status: Spring, summer and fall.

Habitat: Meadows.

Similar Species: The Horned Lark, *Eremophila alpestris* (AS), also displays a prominent black breast crescent, but has horn-like head tufts.

Comments: Not a true lark, but displaying the prominent black crescent of the Horned Lark.

WHIP-POOR-WILL
Caprimulgus vociferus
Length: 9.75-10 inches
Wingspan: 15-16 inches

Grayish brown
Plate 39, No. 2

Description Male: Upper body grayish brown to gray with numerous black markings. Lower body: breast dark gray with thin white band below throat; belly dull yellowish with numerous black markings. Head: cap to back of neck gray with numerous black markings; cheeks dark brown; throat black; bill short, flattened, dark gray. Wings long with rounded tips, a mixture of gray, black, yellowish brown and reddish brown. Tail long, rounded, dark gray, three outer feathers on each side with conspicuous white tips. Legs dark gray.

Discription Female: Similar to male but white on upper breast and tail replaced by dull yellow.

Nesting Season: May - June.

Nest: No nest is built, eggs laid on ground among leaves.

Eggs: Two, dirty white with brown markings, 1.18 inches long by 0.84 inch wide.

Seasonal Status: Spring, summer and fall.

Habitat: Woodland edges.

Similar Species: The Common Nighthawk, *Chordeiles minor* (Sp, S, F), has long, pointed wings with a large white patch that is conspicuous during flight and a somewhat forked tail.

Comments: The Whip-poor-will is named for its mournful evening cry. The Common Nighthawk is most frequently observed after dark above village lights at great heights.

BLACK-BILLED CUCKOO
Coccyzus erythropthalmus
Length: 11-12 inches
Wingspan: 16-17 inches

Brown
Plate 39, No. 4

Description Male: Upper body dull brown. Lower body white. Head dull brown; throat white, eye ring red; bill long, slightly curved and black. Wings dull brown. Tail long, rounded, feathers dull brown with inconspicuous white tips. Legs dark gray.

Description Female: Nearly identical to male.

Nesting Season: June.

Nest: Located in a bush or low tree, loosely constructed of sticks and twigs.

Eggs: Two to five, pale green to greenish blue, 1.14 inches long by 0.8 inch wide.

Seasonal Status: Spring, summer and fall.

Habitat: Thickets and woodland edges.

Similar Species: The Yellow-billed Cuckoo, *C. americanus* (Sp, S, F), has a yellow lower mandible, reddish brown wings and conspicuous white tail spots.

Comments: Previously known as the Rain Crow because it frequently sings loudly just before and during rainy weather. Eats gypsy moths and tent caterpillars.

BROWN THRASHER

Reddish brown
Plate 40, No. 2

Toxostoma rufum

Length: 11-11.5 inches
Wingspan: 12.5-13.5 inches

Description Male: Upper body bright reddish brown. Lower body yellowish white with numerous brown spots. Head reddish brown; throat white; eyes yellow; bill long, curved at tip and dark gray. Wings dark reddish brown with two white shoulder bars. Tail very long, reddish brown. Legs grayish.

Description Female: Similar to the male but paler.

Nesting Season: May - June.

Nest: Located on the ground or in low shrubs, loosely constructed of twigs and grasses.

Eggs: Three to five, dull white to tan with tiny reddish brown spots, 1 inch long by 0.8 inch wide.

Seasonal Status: Spring, summer and fall.

Habitat: Woodlands and fields.

Similar Species: The thrushes may be differentiated from the Brown Thrasher by their smaller sizes, shorter tails and straight bills.

Comments: As its name implies, the Brown Thrasher makes a lot of noise while rustling through dead leaves in search of insects and other food.

HERMIT THRUSH
Catharus guttatus
Length: 7-7.25 inches
Wingspan: 11-12 inches

Brown and white
Plate 40, No. 3

Description Male: Upper body olive brown becoming reddish brown on rump. Lower body: breast white, marked by chains of angular brown spots; belly white with grayish sides. Head olive brown; throat yellowish white marked with brown angular spots; eye ring yellowish; upper mandible dark brown; lower mandible yellowish. Wings olive brown. Tail distinctly reddish brown. Legs brown.

Description Female: Nearly identical to male.

Nesting Season: May - June (a second brood may occur).

Nest: Located on the ground, constructed of leaves, weeds, pine needles and mosses.

Eggs: Three to four, bluish green, 0.88 inch long by 0.69 inch wide.

Seasonal Status: Spring, summer and fall.

Habitat: Mixed woodlands.

Similar Species: No other thrush has a distinctly reddish brown tail. The Wood Thrush, *Hylocichla mustelina* (Sp, S, F), has a reddish brown upper body, a white eye ring and many large, round spots on the breast and belly. The Veery, *C. fuscescens* (Sp, S, F), previously known as Wilson's Thrush, has a rusty brown upper body, lacks a distinct eye ring and has only a few small spots on the upper breast. Swainson's Thrush, *C. ustulatus* (Sp, S, F), has a grayish brown upper body and buffy yellow eye ring and cheeks. The Gray-cheeked Thrush, *C. minimus* (Sp, S, F), has a grayish brown upper body, lacks a distinct eye ring and has gray cheeks.

Comments: Smallest of the thrushes found in the Adirondacks.

GREAT CRESTED FLYCATCHER   Olive brown
Myiarchus crinitis   Plate 41, No. 1
Length: 8-9 inches
Wingspan: 13-14 inches

Description Male: Upper body drab olive brown. Lower body: breast light gray; belly pale sulphur yellow. Head large, crested, olive brown; throat light gray; bill broad, flat and dark gray. Wings brownish with two pale shoulder bars, some feathers with reddish brown edges. Tail reddish brown. Legs dark gray.

Description Female: Nearly identical to male.

Nesting Season: June - July.

Nest: Located in tree cavity or abandoned woodpecker hole, composed of grasses, weeds, feathers, and even shed snake skins.

Eggs: Three to six, pale brown with many purplish brown markings, 0.82 inch long by 0.62 inch wide.

Seasonal Status: Spring, summer and fall.

Habitat: Edges of deciduous woodlands.

Similar Species: No other flycatcher displays a distinct head crest or a reddish brown tail.

Comments: Flycatchers are known for their habit of capturing and feeding on insects during flight.

WILLOW FLYCATCHER   Olive brown
Empidonax traillii   Plate 41, No. 2
Length: 4.75-5 inches
Wingspan: 8.5 inches

Description Male: Upper body drab olive brown to olive gray. Lower body very pale olive brown becoming yellowish towards the tail. Head disproportionately large, olive brown, with a pale eye ring; throat white; bill broad and flat; upper mandible dark brown; lower mandible yellowish. Wings brown with two pale shoulder bars. Tail brown. Legs brown.

Description Female: Nearly identical to male.

Nesting Season: June - July.

Nest: Located in small bushes, composed of grasses, weeds and plant down.

Eggs: Three to four, white with some brown spotting, 0.74 inch long by 0.51 inch wide.

Seasonal Status: Spring, summer and fall.

Habitat: Pastures, orchards and thickets.

Similar Species: The Willow Flycatcher is a member of the genus *Empidonax* which also includes the Yellow-bellied Flycatcher, *E. flaviventris* (Sp, S, F), the Alder Flycatcher, *E. alnorum* (Sp, S, F), and the Least Flycatcher, *E. minimus* (Sp, S, F). These four species have a yellowish lower body, an eye ring and two pale wing bars, making identification based on physical field characteristics nearly impossible. The Eastern Phoebe, *Sayornis phoebe* (Sp, S, F), may display a yellowish breast during fall, but lacks an eye ring. The Olive-sided Flycatcher, *Contopus borealis* (Sp, S, F), has a gray and white lower body and a conspicuous white patch on the lower back. The Eastern Wood Pewee, *C. virens* (Sp, S, F), also has a gray and white lower body but lacks the white rump patch.

Comments: The flycatchers may be identified by their large heads, flat bills and habit of pointing their tails downward when perched.

OVENBIRD   Olive brown
Seiurus aurocapillus   Plate 41, No. 4
Length: 6-6.2 inches
Wingspan: 9.75 inches

Description Male: Upper body, wings and tail pale olive brown. Lower body white with black streaks. Head pale olive brown; crown dull orange; throat white with black streaks; white eye ring; bill pale brown. Legs pale brown.

Description Female: Nearly identical to male.

Nesting Season: June.

Nest: Located on ground, arched over, composed of leaves and grasses.

Eggs: Three to six, off-white with reddish brown markings at larger end, 0.78 inch long by 0.58 inch wide.

Seasonal Status: Spring, summer and fall.

Habitat: Coniferous and deciduous woodlands.

Similar Species: The Northern Waterthrush, *S. noveboracensis* (Sp, S, F), has darker brown plumage and lacks the orange crest. The Ovenbird and Northern Waterthrush may be differentiated from the true thrushes by the presence of streaks, not spots, on the lower body.

Comments: Named for a fanciful resemblance of the nest to old earthen ovens.

BIRDS PREDOMINANTLY OLIVE TO GREEN

OLIVE WARBLERS WITH A STREAKED BELLY

YELLOW WARBLER Olive
Dendroica petechia Plate 42, No. 1 & 2
Length: 4.75-5 inches
Wingspan: 7.8 inches

Description Male: Upper body olive becoming yellowish towards rump. Lower body bright yellow with reddish brown streaks. Head yellow; bill gray. Wings and tail olive brown edged with yellow. Legs brown.

Description Female: Similar to male, but duller and with little or no breast streaking.

Nesting Season: May - June.

Nest: Located in shrubs or small trees, typically 5-10 feet above ground, composed of leaves or grasses, lined with feathers, hair and fern down.

Eggs: Three to five, whitish, sometimes with light bluish or greenish tints, with brownish spots concentrated at the larger end, 0.65 inch long by 0.46 inch wide.

Seasonal Status: Spring, summer and fall.

Habitat: Swampy thickets and orchards.

Similar Species: The Cape May Warbler, *D. tigrina* (Sp, S, F), has darker wings, tail and breast streaks, a chestnut patch about the eyes and a white wing bar.

Comments: The Brown-headed Cowbird often deposits an egg in the nest of the yellow warbler. For additional information see comments under Brown-headed Cowbird.

OLIVE WARBLERS LACKING STREAKED BELLY

COMMON YELLOWTHROAT
Geothlypis trichas
Length: 5-5.3 inches
Wingspan: 7.2 inches

Olive
Plate 42, No. 4

Description Male: Upper body olive green. Lower body bright yellow with a few whitish feathers just forward of the legs. Head dominated by a black mask enclosing forehead, eyes and cheeks; crown and back of neck olive, separated from the black band by a thin, pale gray band; throat bright yellow; bill black. Wings and tail brownish olive. Legs light brown.

Descrition Female: Similar to male, but lacks black facial feathers.

Nesting Season: May - June.

Nest: Located on the ground or in low bushes, typically constructed of coarse grasses and leaves, lined with animal hairs.

Eggs: Four to six, white with fine brown to lilac specks, 0.7 inch long by 0.53 inch wide.

Seasonal Status: Spring, summer and fall.

Habitat: Swampy thickets and shrubby areas.

Similar Species: The Pine Warbler, *Dendroica pinus* (Sp, S, F), has white wing bars and lacks the black facial mask. The Nashville Warbler, *Vermivora ruficapilla* (Sp, S, F), has a light gray head and a yellow throat. The Mourning Warbler, *Oporornis philadelphia* (Sp, S, F), has a gray head and throat and a large black breast patch.

Comments: One of the most common warblers in wooded swamps.

CHESTNUT-SIDED WARBLER
Dendroica pensylvanica
Length: 5-5.25 inches
Wingspan: 7.8-8 inches

Olive
Plate 43, No. 1

Description Male: Upper body a mixture of black and olive streaks. Lower body white; sides of breasts brown to chestnut. Head white; crown yellow; black eye bar; throat white with black edges; bill black. Wing feathers black with white to yellowish markings. Tail blackish with white patches. Legs dark gray.

Description Female: Similar to male, but with a darker crown and less chestnut coloration.

Nesting Season: May - June.

Nest: Located in low bushes, typically 1.5-8 feet above ground, compactly constructed of grasses and thin strips of bark.

Eggs: Two to four, white with reddish brown specks concentrated at the larger end, 0.68 inch long by 0.5 inch wide.

Seasonal Status: Spring, summer and fall.

Habitat: Young woodlands, orchards and thickets.

Similar Species: The Black-throated Green Warbler, *D. virens* (Sp, S, F), has a yellowish olive upper body and head, a black throat and breast, and lacks chestnut coloration.

Comments: One of the most common warblers.

GOLDEN-CROWNED KINGLET
Regulus satrapa
Length: 4 inches
Wingspan: 6.75 inches

Olive
Plate 43, No. 2

Description Male: Upper body olive green. Lower body dull white. Head dull white; crown orange edged with yellow then black, with a white streak above a black eye bar; bill black. Wings greenish brown with two white shoulder bars. Tail greenish brown. Legs black.

Description Female: Similar to male, but crown entirely yellow edged with black.

Nesting Season: April - May.

Nest: Located in the upper reaches of conifer trees, especially spruce, globular, composed of mosses and strips of bark, lined with feathers.

Eggs: Six to ten, dull white with pale brown specks, 0.56 inch long by 0.44 inch wide.

Seasonal Status: Permanent resident.

Habitat: Coniferous forests.

Similar Species: The Ruby-crowned Kinglet, *R. calendula* (Sp, S, F), has a white eye ring and a scarlet crown.

Comments: One of the more common birds of the High Peaks. Consumes many destructive insects.

RED-EYED VIREO
Vireo olivaceus

Olive green
Plate 43, No. 3

Length: 5.75-6.25 inches
Wingspan: 9.5-10.75 inches

Description Male: Upper body olive green to brownish olive. Lower body white with pale olive yellow on sides. Head: cap gray with black margin; dark brown eye bar; area between eye bar and cap margin white; cheeks olive green; throat white; eyes ruby red; upper mandible slightly hooked, dark gray; lower mandible light gray. Wing and tail olive green to brownish olive with darker hues. Legs light gray.

Description Female: Nearly identical to male.

Nesting Season: June (a second brood may occur).

Nest: Suspended from branches of deciduous trees, typically 5-45 feet above ground, constructed of grasses, lichens, spider webs and animal hairs.

Eggs: Three to five, white with a few brown specks at larger end, 0.85 inch long by 0.56 inch wide.

Seasonal Status: Spring, summer and fall.

Habitat: Deciduous and mixed woodlands.

Similar Species: The Solitary Vireo, *V. solitarius* (Sp, S, F), has an olive green upper body, gray head with white eye ring and throat and white lower body and wing bars. The Yellow-Throated Vireo, *V. flavifrons* (Sp, S, F), has an olive green upper body and head, yellow eye ring, throat and breast, and white wing bars. The Warbling Vireo, *V. gilvus* (Sp, S, F), has a grayish to very dull olive brown upper body, head, wings and tail and a dirty white eye bar and lower body.

Comments: No other Vireo has a ruby red eye.

RUBY-THROATED HUMMINGBIRD
Archilochus colubris

Bright green
Plate 44, No. 1 & 2

Length: 3.5-3.75 inches
Wingspan: 4.5 inches

Description Male: Upper body bright metallic green. Lower body grayish white becoming greenish on the sides. Head bright metallic green; throat ruby red; bill long, needle-like, black. Wings greenish brown. Tail deeply forked, greenish brown to violet brown. Legs brown.

Description Female: Similar to male but has a whitish throat and a squarish tail with white-tipped feathers.

Nesting Season: June.

Nest: Located on a tree branch, typically 5-60 feet above ground, constructed of soft plant down, plastered with lichens.

Eggs: Two, white, 0.5 inch long by 0.3 inch wide.

Seasonal Status: Spring, summer and fall.

Habitat: Open fields and woodland edges.

Similar Species: No other hummingbird is found in the Adirondacks.

Comments: The smallest Adirondack bird. It is attracted to gardens containing tubular red to yellowish flowers such as Oswego Tea, Honeysuckle, Nasturtium and Trumpet Creeper. To prepare hummingbird feeder solution at home, dissolve one part white sugar in four parts water (stronger solutions may be harmful). Although traditionally 2-3 drops of red food coloring have been added to attract the birds, this practice is now being disputed by some who feel it is better to have some bright red on the feeder itself. Change feeder solution every other day during periods of hot weather.

BIRDS PREDOMINANTLY ANY SHADE OF YELLOW

AMERICAN GOLDFINCH Yellow and black
Carduelis tristis Plate 44, No. 3
Length: 5-5.2 inches
Wingspan: 9-9.25 inches

Description Male: Upper and lower body bright canary yellow. Head bright canary yellow; crown black; bill flesh-colored. Wings black with white bar-like markings. Tail feathers black, some with white edges. Legs brown. In winter, colored like the female.

Description Female: Upper body and head brownish olive. Lower body yellowish white. Wings and tail feathers black with paler edges.

Nesting Season: July - August.

Nest: Located in trees and shrubs, typically 5-35 feet above ground, compactly constructed of grasses and mosses and lined with plant down.

Eggs: Three to six, pale bluish white, 0.65 inch long by 0.52 inch wide.

Seasonal Status: Permanent resident.

Habitat: Meadows and overgrown pastures.

Similar Species: The Evening Grosbeak, *Coccothraustes vespertinus* (AS), is a much larger bird with a brown head and a stouter bill.

Comments: Associated with thistles which they use for food, shelter and nesting material. The nest is constructed the latest of all our native birds.

EVENING GROSBEAK
Coccothraustes vespertinus
Length: 8 inches
Wingspan: 11.5 inches

Brownish yellow
Plate 44, No. 4

Description Male: Upper and lower body brownish yellow becoming brighter yellow towards the tail. Head olive brown; crown very dark brown, with a yellow handlebar-shaped area above eyes; bill short, conical and yellow. Wings black with large white patch. Tail black. Legs flesh-colored.

Description Female: Upper body, lower body and head brownish gray with yellowish tints. Wings and tail black with white markings.

Nesting Season: June.

Nest: Located in conifer trees, constructed of twigs.

Eggs: Three to four, dull green with pale brown spots, 0.9 inch long by 0.65 inch wide.

Seasonal Status: Permanent resident.

Habitat: Mixed woodlands.

Similar Species: The American Goldfinch, *Carduelis tristis* (AS), is a smaller bird with a yellow, black-capped head and a thinner bill.

Comments: Frequent visitor to bird feeders stocked with sunflower seeds. Absent from the Adirondacks until the early 1900's, its population has been steadily increasing. Often appears in large flocks.

BIRDS PREDOMINANTLY
ANY SHADE OF RED

PINE GROSBEAK   Dull red
Pinicola enucleator   Plate 45, No. 1
Length: 9-9.5 inches
Wingspan: 13-14 inches

Description Male: Upper body dull red with brownish markings between the shoulders. Lower body dull red becoming grayish near tail. Head bright red; bill short, conical and blackish. Wing feathers brown with white edges. Tail forked, brown. Legs blackish.

Description Female: Similar to male but dull red coloration replaced by yellowish hues.

Nesting Season: This bird is not known to breed in the Adirondacks.

Nest: Not applicable.

Eggs: Not applicable.

Seasonal Status: Winter resident.

Habitat: Coniferous woodlands.

Similar Species: The Red Crossbill, *Loxia curvirostra* (AS), is a smaller bird with crossed bill tips and lacks white wing markings.

Comments: Feeds on spruce cones and berries of mountain ash. Shows little fear of humans and can almost be touched if approached slowly.

WHITE-WINGED CROSSBILL   Pinkish red
Loxia leucoptera   Plate 45, No. 2
Length: 6 inches
Wingspan: 10 inches

Description Male: Upper body pinkish red with dark brown streaks. Lower body pinkish red becoming gray near rump. Head pinkish red; bill tips crossed, dark gray. Wings black with two white shoulder bars. Tail forked, black. Legs dark grayish.

Description Female: Upper body and head yellowish with brown streaks. Lower body yellowish gray, streaked with brown. Wings and tail similar to the male.

Nesting Season: March - April.

Nest: Located in coniferous trees at various heights, composed of twigs, birch bark and mosses.

Eggs: Three to four, pale blue to pale green with brown dots, 0.8 inch long by 0.56 inch wide.

Seasonal Status: Permanent resident.

Habitat: Coniferous woodlands.

Similar Species: The Red Crossbill, *L. curvirostra* (AS), has darker red coloration and lacks white wing bars.

Comments: The Adirondacks are close to the southern extent of its normal range.

RED CROSSBILL
Loxia curvirostra

Light red
Plate 45, No. 3

Length: 6.2 inches
Wingspan: 10.75 inches

Description Male: Upper body light red. Lower body light red with gray rump. Head red; bill tips crossed, brown. Wings brown. Tail forked, brown. Legs dark brown.

Description Female: Upper body and head brownish, becoming yellowish on rump. Lower body yellowish. Wings and tail brown.

Nesting Season: March - April.

Nest: Located high up in conifer trees, constructed of bark, twigs, mosses and grasses.

Eggs: Three to four, pale green with brownish spots, 0.83 inch long by 0.55 inch wide.

Seasonal Status: Permanent resident.

Habitat: Coniferous woodlands.

Similar Species: The White-winged Crossbill, *L. leucoptera* (AS), is a paler red and exhibits white wing bars.

Comments: The unusually shaped bill is adapted to extraction of seeds from pine cones. Can easily be approached.

HOUSE FINCH
Carpodacus mexicanus

Dull red and brown
Plate 45, No. 4

Length: 5.25-5.75 inches
Wingspan: 9.5 inches

Description Male: Upper body brown with dull red rump. Lower body: upper breast dull red; lower breast and belly white with prominent brown streaks. Head dull red with brown crown, cheeks and bill. Wings, tail and legs brown.

Description Female: Upper body brown. Lower body white with prominent brown streaks. Head brown; throat white with brown streaks. Wings and tail brown.

Nesting Season: May - June.

Nest: Located in bushes, constructed of twigs and grasses.

Eggs: Three to five, bluish with black spots, 0.8 inch long by 0.6 inch wide.

Seasonal Status: Permanent resident.

Habitat: Edges of woodlands and fields, frequently in towns and villages.

Similar Species: The Purple Finch, *C. purpureus* (AS), lacks the brown crown and brown belly streaks.

Comments: Originally a western species. Adirondack populations descended from caged birds that escaped near New York City around the middle of the 20th century. Some believe the House Finch may be hybridizing with the native Purple Finch.

PURPLE FINCH   Rose red and brown
Carpodacus purpureus   Plate 46, No. 1
Length: 6-6.25 inches
Wingspan: 10 inches

Description Male: Upper body rose red, brightest on rump, with brown markings between shoulders. Lower body rose red shading to grayish white near tail. Head rose red with small brownish area around eyes; bill brown. Wing feathers brown with pinkish gray edges. Tail forked, brown. Legs brown.

Description Female: Upper body and head brown with dark brown streaks. Lower body white with brown markings. Wings and tail brown.

Nesting Season: May - June.

Nest: Located in conifer trees, usually 6-50 feet above ground, composed of small twigs and grasses.

Eggs: Four to six, pale green with black and purple spots, 0.8 inch long by 0.6 inch wide.

Seasonal Status: Permanent resident.

Habitat: Edges of woodlands and fields, frequently in towns and villages.

Similar Species: The House Finch, *C. mexicanus* (AS), has a brown crown and prominent brown belly streaks.

Comments: Often seen at bird feeders.

CARDINAL
Cardinalis cardinalis

Red
Plate 46, No. 2 & 3

Length: 8-8.5 inches
Wingspan: 11-12 inches

Description Male: Upper and lower body bright red. Head conspicuously crested, bright red; throat and region around bill black; bill short, conical, and coral red. Wings and tail red. Legs brown. In winter, wings and tail red tinged with gray.

Description Female: Upper body brownish, brownish gray below, with wings, tail, crest dull red; bill pale to coral red.

Nesting Season: May - June (a second brood may occur).

Nest: Located in bushes, 3-12 feet above ground, constructed of twigs, bark, leaves and grasses.

Eggs: Three to four, white to bluish white or gray, spotted with brown, 1 inch long by 0.7 inch wide.

Seasonal Status: Permanent resident.

Habitat: Woodlands and thickets.

Similar Species: The Scarlet Tanager, *Piranga olivacea* (Sp, S, F), is a smaller bird that lacks a head crest and has black wings and tail.

Comments: Frequently attracted to bird feeders containing sunflower seeds.

SCARLET TANAGER
Piranga olivacea
Length: 7-7.25 inches
Wingspan: 11-12 inches

Scarlet and black
Plate 46, No. 4

Description Male: Upper body, lower body and head brilliant scarlet; bill pale brown. Wings and tail black. Legs brown. In autumn turning the color of the female, but retaining the darker wings and tail.

Description Female: Upper body olive green. Lower body greenish yellow. Wings and tail dull brown.

Nesting Season: June.

Nest: Located in trees, typically 15-35 feet above ground, loosely constructed of small sticks and straws.

Eggs: Three to five, light greenish blue with brown and purplish spotting, 0.95 inch long by 0.65 inch wide.

Seasonal Status: Spring, summer and fall.

Habitat: Woodlands and orchards.

Similar Species: The Cardinal, *Cardinalis cardinalis* (AS), is a larger bird with a crested head, a black face mask, and red wings and tail.

Comments: Perhaps the most brilliantly colored bird in the Adirondacks. Sometimes humorously referred to as a Black-winged Redbird.

NOTES

RARE AND ENDANGERED BIRDS IN NEW YORK STATE

New York State has adopted a series of specific designations and regulations to help protect some of New York's rare birds. All persons spending time out-of-doors are asked to use special care not to harm or disturb the following birds, their nesting sites or their food sources. The most serious of all the designations is "Endangered Species." All species with this heading are believed to be in imminent danger of extinction or extirpation in New York state or are federally listed as endangered. The following birds are listed as "Endangered Species" in New York State.

Bald Eagle	*Haliaeetus leucocephalus* *
Golden Eagle	*Aquila chrysaetos* *
Peregrine Falcon	*Falco peregrinus* *
Piping Plover	*Charadrius melodus*
Eskimo Curlew	*Numenius borealis*
Roseate Tern	*Sterna dougallii*
Least Tern	*Sterna antillarum*
Loggerhead Shrike	*Lanius ludovicianus*

The following birds are listed as "Threatened Species." These are likely to become endangered species within the foreseeable future in New York State or are federally listed as threatened.

Osprey	*Pandion haliaetus*
Northern Harrier	*Circus cyaneus*
Red-shouldered Hawk	*Buteo lineatus*
Spruce Grouse	*Dendragapus canadensis*
Common Tern	*Sterna hirundo*

* The Endangered Species Unit of the New York State Department of Environmental Conservation has requested that sightings of these species be reported to either of the following addresses:

Endangered Species Unit
Wildlife Resources Center
Delmar, NY 12054   Phone: (518) 439-7635

New York State Department of Environmental Conservation
Route 86
Raybrook, NY 12977   Phone: (518) 891-1370

All birds listed as "Special Concern Species" are those native species which are not yet recognized as endangered or threatened but for which documented evidence exists suggesting these birds may deserve the more serious designations in the future. The following are listed as "Special Concern Species":

Common Loon	*Gavia immer*
Least Bittern	*Ixobrychus exilis*
Cooper's Hawk	*Accipiter cooperii*
Black Rail	*Laterallus jamaicensis*
Upland Sandpiper	*Bartramia longicauda*
Black Tern	*Chlidonias niger*
Barn Owl	*Tyto alba*
Short-eared Owl	*Asio flammeus*
Common Nighthawk	*Chordeiles minor*
Common Raven	*Corvus corax*
Sedge Wren	*Cistothorus platensis*
Eastern Bluebird	*Sialia sialis*
Vesper Sparrow	*Pooecetes gramineus*
Grasshopper Sparrow	*Ammodramus savannarum*
Henslow's Sparrow	*Ammodramus henslowii*

Please note that these lists apply to *all* of New York State, not just the Adirondack area.

ATTRACTING BIRDS

Feeding and watching birds is rapidly becoming one of the most popular pastimes. With a little effort, and at a modest cost, you can attract a wide variety of beautiful wild birds to your yard.

The Ideal Environment

Although some species can be attracted to almost any location, the largest number of birds will be attracted to those habitats having the greatest plant diversity. Landscapes that provide a combination of trees and shrubs, colorful flowers, vines and grasses are especially appealing. When selecting plants, consider those that offer cover, protection, and nesting material as well as some that bear fruit during different seasons. Place the tallest trees and shrubs farthest from the house and shorter flowers and vines closer. Whenever possible, include a mixture of conifer and deciduous trees and leave both sunny and shady areas which are appealing to most birds.

Neighborhood Nesting

A nicely landscaped environment with a convenient food and water supply can entice birds to nest nearby. Some breeding pairs can be encouraged to nest in your backyard by providing nesting materials. The following are commonly used in nest construction: dried grass clippings, plant down, pieces of string and yarn, thin strips of cloth, animal hair, lichens and mosses, gauze strips, twigs and mud. Except for mud, which can be offered in a partially buried bowl or pan, nesting materials should be clean and dry. They can be placed in a wire basket and secured to a tree branch or trunk, displayed on a wire or draped over branches of trees and shrubs.

Although most birds build nests in carefully concealed areas in trees, among grasses, in a tree cavity or among dense vegetation, some species will utilize homemade or commercially available birdhouses and nesting shelves. They may be constructed of cardboard, wood, metal, fiberglass, ceramic and other materials. Nesting shelves are partially enclosed platforms that should be located under an eave of a house. Birdhouses may be placed in the open atop a tall pole or post, in shady areas suspended from a sturdy branch, or attached to a tree trunk in a sunny location.

Birdhouses and nesting shelves should be cleaned each fall. Remove all nesting materials and thoroughly wash the shelf or house in preparation for the following spring.

Water Sources

Providing fresh water during all seasons is a key element for attracting birds who can quickly become dependent on a convenient water source. The two most commonly used methods for providing water are birdbaths and shallow garden pools.

Simple birdbaths can be constructed using a garbage can lid or a large shallow pan. Commercially available birdbaths are made of plastic or concrete. Ideally there should be a two to three-foot-wide basin atop a three-foot pedestal, with a gradual, non-slippery slope, and a maximum depth of three inches. It should be cleaned regularly and fresh water should be added daily. A soap-free scouring pad is helpful for removing dirt and algae that accumulate on the inner surface of the bowl. Locate the birdbath in an open area away from shrubs, making it difficult for cats to surprise unwary bathers.

A shallow garden pool can be constructed by placing a large ceramic dish or garbage can lid into a depression dug into the ground. Locate the pool away from shrubs and other garden plants. Small stones can be added to adjust the depth from one to three inches. More elaborate pools may be constructed and often include aquatic plants, fish, liners and filter systems.

Gently running water is especially appealing to some birds. A trickle from a garden hose or sprinkler, or a submersible pump with plastic tubing will provide peaceful sounds that attract many species.

The Art of Feeding Birds

Because diet varies from species to species, a variety of foods needs to be provided, especially during winter months. Not all birds eat seeds, and if you want to attract the non-seed eaters, you will have to offer alternatives such as animal fats or fruits.

Animal fats such as suet and ham fat are excellent sources of energy for birds. Remember that fats spoil quickly in warm weather. Commercially available suet cakes with embedded seeds are very popular at feeding stations.

A variety of inexpensive birdseeds such as cracked corn, millet, wheat, safflower, and sunflower is available commercially and can be obtained by the pound or in bulk quantities. The most popular of these are sunflower seeds. More expensive seeds include Niger seed and peanut hearts. Birdseed mixtures are sold commercially and are available in bags up to fifty pounds or more. Birdseed mixtures have the disadvantage of containing a percentage of less desirable seed types which are frequently discarded by birds searching for their favorites.

Peanut butter is an excellent source of protein and a favorite treat for many birds. One of the best ways to provide it is to use a hole feeder. Use a spatula or knife to fill the drill holes of the feeder.

Nuts are also an excellent source of protein. Almost any commonly available nut can be offered and may be served on the half-shell or shelled. If you are providing expensive nuts in a platform feeder on or near the ground, you should be aware that squirrels will become steady customers.

Many birds are attracted to feeders by a variety of fruits. Apples, oranges, raisins, cherries, cranberries and many others can be provided on platform feeders, placed on the ground or strung on thread and suspended from a branch. Orange halves may also be nailed to a tree branch.

Birds eat many kinds of bakery products, even those that are stale. Examples include breads, cakes, pie crusts, doughnuts, cookies and biscuits. An easy way to serve them is to break them into pieces and scatter them on the ground. Avoid placing too much food at one time because it will attract a variety of other guests and it may spoil.

Many other kinds of foods can serve as treats. Dry dog food is highly nutritious. Corn on-the-cob that has been boiled will sometimes create a feeding frenzy when sections are placed on the ground or in a platform feeder. Popcorn is also popular with some birds and may be offered on the ground, in a platform feeder, or strung on thread and suspended from a tree.

Bird Feeders: Types and Location

When you decide to purchase birdseed, suet or other bird foods, it is important to offer them in appropriate feeders. The construction quality of a feeder and the ease of resupplying food should be considered. Those made of durable materials designed for years of service are the best choices. Some of the most common types of feeders are described below.

Nearly all backyards have a number of natural feeders; most flat surfaces can be used as a feeder. Examples include tree stumps, boulders, fence posts, patios and even the lawn. Do not over feed in these areas because unwanted visitors such as mice and rats will also be attracted.

A platform feeder is a flat surface with a narrow border around it to contain the seeds. It attracts a wide variety of birds because it clearly displays the types of seeds offered. It may be raised slightly off the ground on short legs or elevated several feet. Some platform feeders have a roof and some are divided into compartments. A few small holes drilled into the platform will allow water to drain.

Commercially available tube feeders with tiny holes and perches are excellent for dispensing Niger seed. Six or more smaller birds, such as finches, can be accommodated at the same time. The tube feeder is specifically designed to slowly dispense seed and to keep it dry. Large birds find it difficult to obtain seeds from tube feeders.

Hopper feeders have a roof and come in a wide variety of sizes and shapes. They are usually constructed of wood, plastic or metal. Seeds are dispensed by gravity into an accessible feeding tray.

Window feeders are platform or hopper feeders that offer the advantage of attracting birds very close to your house. Because of their location they are easy to resupply and clean. However, many species will not visit window feeders because they prefer to feed at a greater distance from the house. Some of the most common Adirondack birds that will visit are the House Finch, Goldfinch and Black-capped Chickadee.

Hole feeders are excellent for providing peanut butter, cheeses and bits of fruit. To make one, cut a three to four-inch diameter log to approximately two feet. Using a one-inch spade bit, drill one-inch deep holes at various heights on the log and insert an eye screw or hammer a nail into one end. Use a piece of wire or string to suspend the feeder from a branch or a crossbar of a feeder station atop a post or pole.

Suet is a rich source of animal fat that can be offered in a variety of ways. One of the most popular suet feeders is a wire basket that can be tied to or suspended from a tree or post. If you provide suet during the warmer months, be sure to offer small quantities and check it regularly to assure freshness.

Several factors should be considered when deciding where to locate bird feeders. They may be hung from tree branches, affixed to windows or window ledges, erected on posts or poles, mounted on tree trunks or placed on the ground. Select a safe location away from plantings where cats won't be able to hide. Feeders should be placed where you can see the birds and should be accessible for resupplying and cleaning.

Backyard Pests and Household Hazards

One of the most serious problems for birds in your backyard is neighborhood cats. To reduce this problem, place feeders and bird baths 15-20 feet from vegetation.

Rabbits are fond of birdseed and can be frequent visitors to feeder stations with ample seeds on the ground. The fact that they consume seed on the ground is wonderful and enjoyable to watch. The problem however, is that they may also be attracted to your vegetable garden. Fencing may need to be installed to protect your garden.

Squirrels present a truly unique problem at feeders. They may be enjoyable to observe for a while, but when they discover how to access a feeder the fascination stops and trouble begins. They can sit in the feeding tray of a hopper feeder or in a platform feeder for hours while consuming large quantities of food and keeping birds at bay. One of the most economical and practical ways to deny squirrels access to a feeder is to use aluminum flashing that is placed between the feeder and the squirrel. For post or pole mounted feeders, wrap a two to three-foot-long piece of aluminum flashing around the post or pole at a height of three to four feet off the ground. For hanging feeders, use aluminum flashing overlapped to form a cone and place it several feet abofe the feeder.

Finally, humans can be a problem for birds in your backyard. Baby birds and nests should *never* be handled and birdhouses should never be disturbed in any manner.

PHOTOGRAPHING BIRDS

On a cold, late afternoon in March, the Pileated Wood-pecker flew to its roosting hole high in a beech tree. As the bird raised its prominent red crest, I fired the camera via a remote control unit and hoped that the image obtained was the same as in my mind's eye. For almost four months I had followed this particular bird to learn its habits. On this day the camera and flash unit were placed on a brace approximately 40 feet high in an adjacent tree. The telephoto lens was prefocused on the roosting hole that this magnificent woodpecker seemed to prefer. I was located on the ground with a remote control unit camouflaged by sitting beneath a small hemlock. When the Pileated flew to the tree, it investigated two roosting holes prior to going to the hole on which the camera had been pre-focused. At the moment the woodpecker was in its best posi-tion, the remote unit was triggered, firing both the camera and flash.

With the recent proliferation of 35mm cameras coupled with the increasing appeal of birding as a recreational activity, the popularity of bird photography cannot be far behind. The example of the Pileated Woodpecker is perhaps reflective of a higher level of commitment than would be required by the typical bird photographer. However, it does point out some essential elements of this challenging hobby.

The first question usually asked is what type of equipment is needed for bird photography. In general, a well-rounded outfit would include a 35mm camera with a motor drive/winder, a 90-105mm macro lens, a 300-400mm telephoto lens, a sturdy tripod and binoculars. Accessories should include at least one strobe, various clamps, PC cords or slaves, cable release, and some type of remote control unit. The choice of film is depen-dent upon several factors including, but not limited to, the film speed, color rendition, and graininess. In general, the slower the film speed the more detail and color saturation can be obtained. However, if working with natural light, slow films often do not offer the photographer the advantage of using the fast shutter speeds often needed for freezing movement. The aspiring photographer should be aware that most publishers prefer slower slide films since they transfer most accurately and easily onto the printed page.

Whether taking photographs in the field or in your own backyard, an aesthetically pleasing background adds tremendously to the final photograph. Knowing a bird's natural habitat can help the photographer choose an angle which will best represent the bird's surroundings. For example, yellow warblers frequent open country with scattered saplings and hedgerows. Hummingbirds often nest near a stream on a downward sloping branch with a canopy of leaves directly above the nest. Some birds such as the Saw-whet Owl prefer mixed conifer and hardwood in the summer while they will usually be found in small dense stands of only conifers in the winter.

Finding a nest is sometimes a difficult task. Depending on the species, the photographer should be able to observe the male singing. Watch for telltale signs of nesting such as the bird carrying nesting material or food for its young. If you are able to follow the direction it is heading, the nest should be able to be found through further observation.

There are three basic methods of photographing birds. These include shooting from a blind, stalking and the use of remote control. Of these three types, working from a blind is probably the best overall method. A blind can be anything which effectively hides the photographer from the bird. It can be as simple as camouflage material draped over the photographer or as sophisticated as scaffolding with a tent-like structure on top. A good all purpose blind should be fairly portable, tall enough to stand in and have provisions for taking pictures from various heights within the structure. An often overlooked but excellent blind is your automobile.*

Two excellent locations for a blind are either in close proximity to a nest or feeding station. Generally a telephoto lens of approximately 300-400mm placed on a tripod works best when shooting from a blind. It is preferable to photograph a nest site after the young have hatched; the adult birds have a much stronger bond after the eggs have hatched and are therefore less likely to abondon the nest. Once a nest is found, the blind

---

*The March/April 1987 edition of *The Conservationist* contains an excellent article by Dave Spier on photographing wildlife from your car.

should be moved closer to it over a period of time so the birds can gradually get used to its presence. Birds build their nests in the most advantageous situations in order to protect themselves from both the elements and predators. Because of this it is not a good idea to permanently remove branches or leaves for a photograph. If necessary, a branch can be temporarily tied back with a string and later replaced to its original location.

The other excellent location for a blind is near bird feeders, especially in winter. Through observation the photographer can determine where a particular bird lands prior to flying to the feeder. If no branches are present near the feeder, it is a good idea to either move the feeder closer to cover or "set up" a few branches in close proximity to the feeder. The feeders and branches should be placed in positions which have a good background and are well lit for a good part of the day.

Remote control photography can be done near feeders particularly if a small area on a given branch is often used by the bird(s) before flying to the feeder. However, remote control is used to its greatest advantage at a nest site. This technique is achieved by placing the camera on a tripod and prefocusing on the spot where, through observation, it is determined the bird is most likely to land when feeding its young. The camera is triggered by the photographer via some type of remote control unit. The photographer in most instances can sit some distance from the nest while observing with binoculars. A macro lens of approximately 100mm is an excellent choice for this type of photography. If the nest is found in a location which receives little sunlight, this situation requires the use of strobes. A good method to use with strobes is a main flash above and 45 degrees off the camera. A less powerful flash is placed close to the camera and is used as a fill light. The placement of the strobes can be accomplished by the use of clamps or a second tripod. The exposure should be calculated from the distance the main flash is from the subject. Birds are sometimes skittish during the first few flashes but most soon become accustomed to both the flash and noise of the camera.

Stalking is a rather difficult method since it is usually not possible to walk close enough to a bird to capture a frame-filling shot. This is generally true because the bird views the stalking photographer as a predator and will take flight while quite a distance away. There are some tricks that can be used to help improve a photographer's chances. When approaching a bird, the photographer should take an indirect rather than a direct line and only move when the bird seems disinterested in your presence. It is also a good idea not to make eye contact since this will only enhance the bird's instinctual fear of predators. If stalking in the woods or secondary growth, camouflage clothing is an advantage since it can break up the outline of a human figure. A shoulder stock to help in steadying a camera with a telephoto lens can be a great help in this situation.

A very good friend once told me, "It's not a picture until it's a picture." There are many variables in bird photography, any one of which can ruin the photograph. Exposure, focusing, processing, battery failure, and many other variables are just some of the things that can go wrong. Luckily for me, on that cold March day, my picture of the Pileated Woodpecker came back just the way I had visualized it, thereby giving me the remainder of the winter to pursue the Snowy Owl.

—Warren S. Greene

Killdeer
Charadrius vociferus

VISUAL GLOSSARY

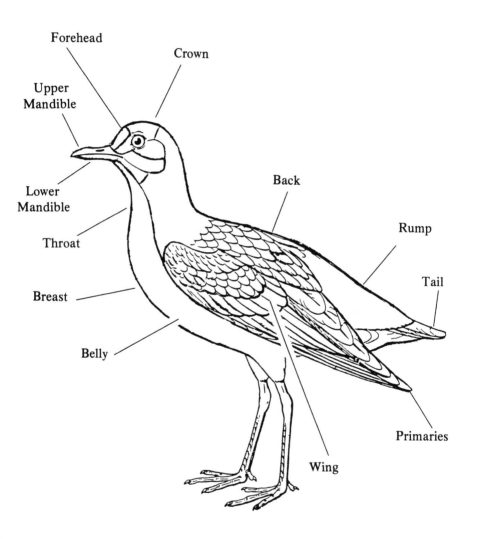

Forehead

Crown

Upper
Mandible

Lower
Mandible

Throat

Breast

Belly

Back

Rump

Tail

Primaries

Wing

GLOSSARY

Arched over	A canopy-like extension covering the nest.
Avian	Pertaining to birds.
Barred	Marked by alternating and contrasting bars of color perpendicular to the length of the body or feather.
Base	That portion of a feather, wing, tail or bill directly joined to the body.
Boreal	Pertaining to the coniferous forests found in the northern areas of the continent.
Breast	The portion of the lower body between the throat and belly.
Cap	Generalized term referring to the crown and upper sides of the head.
Chevron	A V-shaped marking.
Collar	A band of color encircling the neck.
Conical	More or less shaped like a cone.
Conifer	A cone-bearing tree such as a pine or spruce, typically with evergreen needle-like leaves.
Coniferous	Pertaining to conifer trees.
Crest	An ornamental tuft of feathers on the top and back of the head.
Crown	The top of the head, often distinctly colored.
Deciduous	Referring to any tree or shrub with broad flat leaves which are shed each autumn, such as maple or oak.
Down	Soft, fibrous material of either plant or avian origin.
Extirpate	To completely remove or destroy an animal population from a given area.
Eye bar	A horizontal bar typically extending in front of and behind the eye.
Eye ring	A circular band of color surrounding the eye.
Forehead	The area between the bill and crown.
Forewing	That portion of the wing furthermost from the body, including the primary flight feathers.
Incomplete webbing	Partial webbing around the toes, seen on grebes and coots, not joining the toes as on ducks.

Mandible	The upper or lower portion of the bill.
Margin	The outermost portion, such as the edge of a feather.
Mask	A strongly contrasting facial patch enclosing the eyes.
Migratory visitant	A species present only during spring and fall migrations.
Mobbing	Several birds of one species harassing one or more birds of a different species.
Mottled	Having a mixture of differently colored spots and blotches.
Permanent resident	A species found throughout the year.
Piebald	Spotted or blotched with different colors, typically black and white and asymmetrical.
Plumage	Feathers.
Primary	The longest flight feathers of the forewing.
Ruff	A collar-like tuft of feathers around the neck.
Rump	The hindquarters of the bird.
Shaft	The quill-like center of a feather.
Shoulder	The area where the wing and body meet.
Speculum	A distinct patch of color located on the trailing edge of the upper wing, present on ducks.
Spur	A claw-like growth on the posterior surface of the foot.
Terminal	Outermost.
Tuft	A protruding cluster of feathers.
Variegated	Having an intricate pattern of discrete and different colors.
Visitant	A nonresident species occasionally observed.
Wattle	A featherless fleshy tissue found on the head or neck of some upland game birds, becoming red and swollen during breeding season.
Webbing	Skin connecting the toes of waterfowl.

INDEX OF COMMON NAMES

INDEX OF SCIENTIFIC NAMES

234

236

ADIRONDACK BIRDS CHECKLIST

To assist the reader in locating species, the birds are presented in the order in which they appear in the book.

Birds of Prey
- [ ] Bald Eagle
- [ ] Golden Eagle
- [ ] Osprey
- [ ] Rough-legged Hawk
- [ ] Red-tailed Hawk
- [ ] Broad-winged Hawk
- [ ] Red-shouldered Hawk
- [ ] Cooper's Hawk
- [ ] Sharp-shinned Hawk
- [ ] Northern Goshawk
- [ ] Marsh Hawk
- [ ] Gyrfalcon
- [ ] Peregrine Falcon
- [ ] American Kestrel
- [ ] Merlin
- [ ] Turkey Vulture
- [ ] Black Vulture

Owls
- [ ] Snowy Owl
- [ ] Great Horned Owl
- [ ] Long-eared Owl
- [ ] Short-eared Owl
- [ ] Hawk-owl
- [ ] Great Gray Owl
- [ ] Barred Owl
- [ ] Eastern Screech Owl
- [ ] Northern Saw-whet Owl
- [ ] Boreal Owl

Waterfowl
- [ ] Tundra Swan
- [ ] Mute Swan
- [ ] Canada Goose
- [ ] Brant
- [ ] Snow Goose
- [ ] Wood Duck
- [ ] Gadwall

- [ ] Mallard
- [ ] Northern Shoveler
- [ ] Blue-winged Teal
- [ ] Green-winged Teal
- [ ] American Wigeon
- [ ] Northern Pintail
- [ ] Oldsquaw
- [ ] Canvasback
- [ ] Redhead
- [ ] Ring-necked Duck
- [ ] Lesser Scaup
- [ ] Greater Scaup
- [ ] Common Goldeneye
- [ ] Barrow's Goldeneye
- [ ] Bufflehead
- [ ] Common Eider
- [ ] Ruddy Duck
- [ ] Hooded Merganser
- [ ] Common Merganser
- [ ] Red-breasted Merganser

Shore and Water Birds
- [ ] Common Loon
- [ ] Double-crested Cormorant
- [ ] Ring-billed Gull
- [ ] Herring Gull
- [ ] Common Tern
- [ ] Black Tern
- [ ] Glossy Ibis
- [ ] Cattle Egret
- [ ] Great Egret
- [ ] Great Blue Heron
- [ ] Little Blue Heron
- [ ] Black-crowned Night-Heron
- [ ] Yellow-crowned Night-Heron
- [ ] Green-backed Heron
- [ ] American Bittern
- [ ] Least Bittern
- [ ] Virginia Rail

Shore and Water Birds *(cont'd)*
- [ ] Sora
- [ ] King Rail
- [ ] Common Moorhen
- [ ] American Coot
- [ ] Pied-billed Grebe
- [ ] Horned Grebe
- [ ] Killdeer
- [ ] Semipalmated Plover
- [ ] Spotted Sandpiper
- [ ] Upland Sandpiper
- [ ] Sanderling

Upland Game Birds
- [ ] American Woodcock
- [ ] Common Snipe
- [ ] Wild Turkey
- [ ] Ring-necked Pheasant
- [ ] Green Pheasant
- [ ] Ruffed Grouse
- [ ] Spruce Grouse
- [ ] Gray Partridge
- [ ] Rock Dove
- [ ] Mourning Dove

Woodpeckers
- [ ] Pileated Woodpecker
- [ ] Common Flicker
- [ ] Black-backed Woodpecker
- [ ] Three-toed Woodpecker
- [ ] Yellow-bellied Sapsucker
- [ ] Red-headed Woodpecker
- [ ] Downy Woodpecker
- [ ] Hairy Woodpecker

Swifts and Swallows
- [ ] Barn Swallow
- [ ] Tree Swallow
- [ ] Purple Martin
- [ ] Cliff Swallow
- [ ] Bank Swallow
- [ ] Northern Rough-winged Swallow
- [ ] Chimney Swift

Perching Birds
- [ ] American Crow

- [ ] Common Raven
- [ ] Common Grackle
- [ ] Rusty Blackbird
- [ ] European Starling
- [ ] Red-winged Blackbird
- [ ] Brown-headed Cowbird
- [ ] Rose-breasted Grosbeak
- [ ] Rufous-sided Towhee
- [ ] Eastern Kingbird
- [ ] Bobolink
- [ ] Black and White Warbler
- [ ] Blackburnian Warbler
- [ ] Northern Oriole
- [ ] American Redstart
- [ ] American Robin
- [ ] Northern Shrike
- [ ] Loggerhead Shrike
- [ ] Gray Jay
- [ ] Mockingbird
- [ ] Catbird
- [ ] Tufted Titmouse
- [ ] Dark-eyed Junco
- [ ] Black-capped Chickadee
- [ ] Boreal Chickadee
- [ ] White-breasted Nuthatch
- [ ] Red-breasted Nuthatch
- [ ] Magnolia Warbler
- [ ] Yellow-rumped Warbler
- [ ] Northern Parula
- [ ] Canada Warbler
- [ ] Black-throated Blue Warbler
- [ ] Bluebird
- [ ] Indigo Bunting
- [ ] Blue Jay
- [ ] Belted Kingfisher
- [ ] Cedar Waxwing
- [ ] Bohemian Waxwing
- [ ] Brown Creeper
- [ ] Lapland Longspur
- [ ] House Wren
- [ ] Winter Wren
- [ ] Long-billed Marsh Wren
- [ ] Short-billed Marsh Wren
- [ ] Song Sparrow
- [ ] Savannah Sparrow
- [ ] Vesper Sparrow

Perching Birds *(cont'd)*
- [ ] Fox Sparrow
- [ ] Chipping Sparrow
- [ ] Field Sparrow
- [ ] Tree Sparrow
- [ ] Swamp Sparrow
- [ ] Grasshopper Sparrow
- [ ] White-throated Sparrow
- [ ] White-crowned Sparrow
- [ ] House Sparrow
- [ ] Pine Siskin
- [ ] Common Redpoll
- [ ] Hoary Redpoll
- [ ] Snow Bunting
- [ ] Horned Lark
- [ ] Eastern Meadowlark
- [ ] Whip-poor-will
- [ ] Common Nighthawk
- [ ] Black-billed Cuckoo
- [ ] Yellow-billed Cuckoo
- [ ] Brown Thrasher
- [ ] **Hermit Thrush**
- [ ] Wood Thrush
- [ ] Swainson's Thrush
- [ ] Gray-cheeked Thrush
- [ ] Veery
- [ ] Great Crested Flycatcher
- [ ] Willow Flycatcher
- [ ] Yellow-bellied Flycatcher
- [ ] Alder Flycatcher

- [ ] Least Flycatcher
- [ ] Olive-sided Flycatcher
- [ ] Eastern Phoebe
- [ ] Eastern Wood Peewee
- [ ] Ovenbird
- [ ] Northern Waterthrush
- [ ] Yellow Warbler
- [ ] Cape May Warbler
- [ ] Common Yellowthroat
- [ ] Pine Warbler
- [ ] Nashville Warbler
- [ ] Mourning Warbler
- [ ] Chestnut-sided Warbler
- [ ] Black-throated Green Warbler
- [ ] Golden-crowned Kinglet
- [ ] Ruby-crowned Kinglet
- [ ] Red-eyed Vireo
- [ ] Solitary Vireo
- [ ] Yellow-throated Vireo
- [ ] Warbling Vireo
- [ ] Ruby-throated Hummingbird
- [ ] American Goldfinch
- [ ] **Evening Grosbeak**
- [ ] Pine Grosbeak
- [ ] White-winged Crossbill
- [ ] Red Crossbill
- [ ] House Finch
- [ ] Purple Finch
- [ ] Cardinal
- [ ] Scarlet Tanager

About the Authors . . .

Alan E. Bessette is professor of biology at Utica College of Syracuse University. His areas of research interest include the morphology and taxonomy of mushrooms, lichens, plants and birds. He is well known as a nature photographer specializing in macrophotography. His interest in birds dates back to his high school days as a native Vermonter, where he began raising and studying birds and learned skills in attracting birds to backyard feeders. Dr. Bessette is a naturalist for the Appalachian and Adirondack Mountain Clubs, advisor to the Mid York Mycological Society, and identification consultant for the New York State Poison Control Center. He is the author of over twenty scientific papers and several books.

William K. Chapman is a biology teacher and member of the adjunct faculty at Utica College of Syracuse University. He is a nature photographer who counts birds of prey and waterfowl among his favorite subjects. Mr. Chapman's published works include *Pheasants Under Glass*; *Hickory, Chicory and Dock*; *Plants and Flowers: An Archival Sourcebook*; and two Adirondack field guides. He has also created *Birds 'n' Butterflies* and *Birds 'n' Blooms* for young naturalists.

Warren Greene is a well-known nature photographer from upstate New York and is the principal photographer for this guide. His greatest interest is bird photography, and he is also an accomplished macro and scenic photographer. Warren's work has appeared in several national field guides, books, and magazines. Regional magazines that have published his work include *Adirondack Life*, *Mohawk Valley*, and *The Conservationist*. Many of his bird photographs have been accepted at the Academy of National Sciences in Philadelphia and the Laboratory of Ornithology at Cornell University. Warren presents programs about birds to numerous New York State clubs and organizations. He resides in Gloversville with his wife Jeanne and their two sons, Stephen and Jacob.

Doug Pens teaches ecology and biology at New Hartford High School and runs the school's Environmental Studies program at Raquette Lake. An avid naturalist, hiker, mountaineer, kayaker, and scuba diver, Doug is also a Wildlife Rehabilitator for the State of New York specializing in the care of owls and birds of prey. He is a recipient of the EPA Environmental Achievement Award and was selected NYS Outstanding Biology Teacher of the Year by the National Association of Biology Teachers. He resides in Clinton, New York with his wife Eileen, and children Amy, Chad and Matt.